STICKS & STONES

The Discipleship of Our Speech

William R. Baker

InterVarsity Press
Downers Grove, Illinois

InterVarsity Press® is the book-publishing division of InterVarsity Christian Fellowship®, a student movement active on campus at hundreds of universities, colleges and schools of nursing in the United States of America, and a member movement of the International Fellowship of Evangelical Students. For information about local and regional activities, write Public Relations Dept., InterVarsity Christian Fellowship, 6400 Schroeder Rd., P.O. Box 7895, Madison, WI 53707-7895.

All Scripture quotations, unless otherwise indicated, are taken from the HOLY BIBLE, NEW INTERNATIONAL VERSION® NIV®. Copyright ©1973, 1978, 1984 by International Bible Society. Used by permission of Zondervan Publishing House. All rights reserved.

Cover illustration: Margo Thompson/SIS

ISBN 0-8308-1986-X

Printed in the United States of America ♾

Library of Congress Cataloging-in-Publication Data

Baker, William R.
  Sticks and Stones/William R. Baker.
    p. cm.
    Includes bibliographical references.
    ISBN 0-8303-1986-X (alk. paper)
    1. Clean speech. 2. Oral communication—Religious aspects—
Christianity. 3. Conversation—Religious aspects—Christianity.
I. Title.
BV4597.53.C64B35 1996
241'.672—dc20   *96-8120*
                                                                                         CIP

20	19	18	17	16	15	14	13	12	11	10	9	8	7	6	5	4	3	2	1
11	10	09	08	07	06	05	04	03	00	02	01	00	99	98	97	96			

To Joni, Gavin and Kyle

Prologue

My first memorable lesson in speech ethics came in first grade. As I whispered to John at a neighboring desk, I looked up to see Mrs. Kluberg standing over me. I don't remember what she said, but I will never forget what she did. She raised her hand and slapped me across the face.

To say the least, I didn't speak to John anymore that day. Whether or not she was right in her method, Mrs. Kluberg did etch into my mind the basic life principle that there are rights and wrongs about speech.

Another lesson in speech ethics came when I was in high school. The day after a weekend youth-group trip that I had enjoyed immensely, I received a phone call from the woman who had driven us. She took me to task for saying something derogatory about her son. I genuinely liked this woman and admired her son. To this day I don't know what she was talking about and can only guess that something I said in jest got twisted around.

As I reflect on this traumatic incident, I realize that it demonstrates an underlying assumption of speech ethics: we can hurt one another by what we say. The woman was hurt because she thought I had derided her son. I, in turn, was hurt because she lashed out at me.

I have no doubt that given a moment's reflection, you could recall vivid circumstances like these two. We can't grow up in this world and have contact with other people without learning valuable lessons about our talk as we go along. Neither can we grow up without being hurt at times by the talk of others.

As adults, we count ourselves fortunate when we can think back on our day and realize it was not marred by speech miscues of one sort or another. When we are aware of having spoken wrongly, we can kick ourselves, feel bad and then start all over the next day. But that doesn't accomplish much. We Christians need to face our speech sins squarely as an ongoing spiritual problem that undermines our call to holiness. We also need to see that the Bible offers solutions that can be organized into a biblical ethics of talk.

That's what this book is about. It provides tangible, biblical help to implement spiritual growth in our talk. Can we do anything to improve our talk? Indeed we can!

A biblical ethics of talk encourages us to minimize the hurt we cause through our speech and provides guidelines for how to speak in helpful ways. This book will discuss controlling anger and lying, the dynamics of talking to God, and learning to listen. It will identify the prominent ways we sin in our speech and suggest spiritual remedies based on biblical principles. Above all, it will call you to real change.

Biblical ethics of talk, or personal speech ethics, has to do with ethics or morality as applied to interpersonal communication. Simply put, it is the rights and wrongs of what we say to one another. The ethics of speech covers when to speak, how to speak and to whom to speak as well as when, how and to whom *not* to speak. It involves the process of human speech and its relationship to thoughts and actions. Fundamentally, speech ethics is about you and me and how our ways of talking to each other impact not only how well we get along but also how successful we are and how much we enjoy life.

Sources for Speech Ethics
Talk fills our lives. Family, friends, coworkers, neighbors, news and sports reports, salespeople, teachers, politicians and preachers knit together the fabric of our lives with talk. Sometimes harmful, sometimes helpful, sometimes pointless, sometimes inane, sometimes cherished, sometimes

too loud, sometimes life-changing, talk is a part of our lives from day to day, year to year.

We learn grammar. We take a speech class. We talk. But crucial as talk is to our lives, most of us don't receive any formal training in the ethics of talk.

What we do learn about the ethics of what to say and what not to say comes by trial and error. Our parents and teachers discipline us when we say what we shouldn't. They encourage us to say "Thank you." They model speech. As we grow, our peers steer our speech in various directions. Through all this we may learn that lying is wrong, but we may also learn that in certain situations lying is perfectly normal. We may discover that making fun of someone is acceptable and even exciting—unless the object of ridicule is ourselves. We may conclude that talking behind someone's back is wrong, or we may find that it is a great way to help us get ahead.

Learning by trial and error has its place, but it's pretty inefficient and unreliable. What can we do if we want to make a concerted effort to improve our talk? Where can we go for help? What sources can help us learn speech ethics?

We are not going to find much help in our contemporary culture. Western culture prides itself on advancements in technology. We have learned to do many things faster and more efficiently. We can launch a space laboratory. We can make amazing cars and computers. We can cure diseases. Despite these kinds of advances, presidents and other political leaders still lie to us, and we lie to one another. We still trade insults. Wars rage because people won't apologize. No progress has been made in the ethics of talk. If anything, the situation is worse.

Not only have we not improved our speech ethics, but we don't even consider it worthy of serious reflection. In a book entitled *Lying*, Sissela Bok notes the complete absence of reference to or any article on lying or deception in the eight-volume *Encyclopedia of Philosophy*.[1] Further scanning for an article on truthfulness, trust or veracity comes up empty as well. How are any of us to make progress in speech ethics or even be concerned, if no one is writing or thinking about the topic?

Well, we can look back at the days of the Bible. Back then, the ethics of talk was a serious subject of study and contemplation. All the great Greek philosophers—Plato, Aristotle, Philo, Epictetus and especially Plutarch—wrote with enormous concern and insight about it. Jewish apocryphal writings like Sirach and Wisdom of Solomon record hundreds of treasured proverbs about speech ethics, while the voice of rabbi after rabbi in rabbinic collections like *Pirqe Abot,* the Midrash and the Talmud teach about the rights and wrongs of various kinds of speech. And, of course, there is the Bible itself, especially the wisdom books like Proverbs, Job, Ecclesiastes and many of the Psalms, but also the thoughts and influence of Jesus in the New Testament. Here we have the inspired foundation for an ethics of talk.

Even earlier than the Old Testament and classical Greek writings are works from Egypt and Babylon. Many of these are among the earliest written documents known to humankind. The oldest among them is "The Instruction of Vizier Ptah-hotep," from Egypt, written as early as 2400 B.C. Another from Egypt, "The Instruction of Meri-Ka-Re," was written about 2100 B.C., and "The Counsels of Wisdom," from Babylonia, was written between 1500 and 1200 B.C. In each of these writings a king or king's adviser outlines the keys to his success to his son or successor, using proverbs and memorable illustrations. The heart and soul of the advice revolves around proper and wise speech. Ptah-hotep advises, "Teach him first about speaking,"[2] and warns, "Speech is more difficult than any craft."[3]

These ancients understood something we don't; a sound ethics of talk grounds success and happiness in life. It's where our education should begin. So we have much to learn from ancient sources, and they will be used in this book. Their preservation over four thousand years is surely due to the basic, universal wisdom they contain.

A Lost Emphasis

The great concern for speech ethics that characterized the people of Bible times—Greek, Jewish and Christian—reflected the predominance of the spoken word as their primary means of communication. They valued what was spoken between individuals more than what might be written. Indeed, the vast majority of people simply were not trained to read and write, as they are today in Western culture. Reading and writing were left to professionally educated individuals. Also, the ancients believed that written words were more subject to misunderstanding and useful for deception than face-to-face communication. It is the rare individual who can lie straight-faced, eye to eye.

The ancients' emphasis on the spoken word is still admirable, but it is not reflected in our education today. Legally, the concept of an oral contract still exists. However, in today's business deals and personal contracts, we rely on written, legal documents as authoritative. Our culture is much more interested in training people in grammar and interpretation than in teaching the morals of talk.

The ancients have something to teach us because they realized more than we do that speech is the fabric of society and that improvement in society requires improvement in speech ethics. They realized that a person's speech connects to the inner core of his or her being. We cannot sever the relationship between what we say and who we are—what we are really like. Jesus' most poignant statement about speech ethics expresses this truth. In Matthew 12:34-35, after the Pharisees accuse him of casting out demons by drawing on the power of Satan, he turns to them and says,

> You brood of vipers, how can you who are evil say anything good? For out of the overflow of the heart the mouth speaks. The good man brings good things out of the good stored up in him, and the evil man brings evil things out of the evil stored up in him.

This teaching represents the wealth of wisdom about the ethics of talk that is stored in the Bible. As we focus on what the Bible has to say about talk, we will uncover a great storehouse of help that you may not have realized was there, simply because you may have never read the Bible looking for it. We will discover astute teaching that will improve the spiritual quality of our everyday lives, transforming our relationships with others and with God. We will be challenged to put our Christian faith to work in our homes, neighborhoods and places of employment. Improving what we say and learning what not to say will transform our world and will produce new vitality in our life with God.

Learning How to Speak

With this book, I hope to guide you in developing an ethic of talk and encourage you to move toward real-life improvement in this basic element of your Christian growth. Our spotlight will be fall on the Bible and what it has to say, but its teaching will be supplemented by wise words from other relevant ancient sources of Hebrew, Greek and occasionally even Egyptian and Babylonian cultures. These do not have anything like the authority of the Bible for us, but they can and will help us understand what the Bible says as well as deepen our understanding of ourselves and our talk.

We will begin by recognizing the power our words have in chapter one, before moving on to identify the ways we sin by what we say in chapters two and three. Chapter four develops the idea of control as the crucial component in speech ethics which provides the opportunity to listen (chapter five) and then speak graciously (chapter six). In chapter seven, speech ethics will be applied to our talks with God. Finally, chapter eight will explore the dynamic interplay between words and action.

1

Speech Is Powerful

*W*hen Ronald Reagan was president of the United States, the media christened him the Great Communicator. His speeches had a powerful impact on his audience. He convinced. He always had a great line for the evening news. He came across as genuine and full of conviction. He dominated opinion in the United States for eight years.

It didn't matter that critics said that Reaganomics shot the federal deficit through the roof or that Reagan tried to sidestep congressional law to aid the contras in Nicaragua. It didn't matter that hundreds of his appointees were brought before grand juries for violations of their office. The power of Reagan's speech kept him unscathed from it all and profoundly shaped U.S. domestic and foreign policy. His words influenced people around the country and around the world.

Saddam Hussein, president of Iraq, presents a notable contrast to Ronald Reagan. It is difficult to judge how powerful his words would be if his rule were not a military dictatorship. The fact that all potential rivals to his position have been executed demonstrates his brute power and his own insecurity in his ability to persuade the Iraqi people with words alone. Using the power of his position, he could send thousands of armed soldiers to invade a defenseless Kuwait, but he could not prevent mass surrender in the face of the coalition forces. He tried to wage a war of words with President George Bush. But Saddam's words rang hollow. His war cry, "the mother of all wars," became the joke heard round the world.

Words can be powerful, but not all words are. This is true of the words of presidents, but it is also the case with your words and mine. My words fall flat if they fail to convince you. Saddam's words convinced no one, not even his own people. Reagan convinced the American people over and over again.

The first amendment to the U.S. Constitution grants every citizen the right of free speech. This is crucial to a democratic society. Words are the seed of change. They bring down corruption and undergird good policy. The Constitution recognizes that free speech is not a threat to good government, only to bad. People can say anything they want, but their words have no power unless they convince others. And the odds are that if they convince so many others that a change is brought about, it is a needed change, whether it be a new elected official or a new policy.

The Bible and the Ancients

The Bible recognizes the power of words. Its very first page tells of words that produced the universe. God spoke the word *light,* and day and night were created. He spoke other words, and earth was separated from the sky, water and land were separated, and the sun, moon and stars appeared. God called for trees, plants, animals and fish, and all came into being. God declared the results of these spoken words "good."

God gave the power of speech to the first man and woman, and apparently also to the serpent. Not long afterward, as Genesis 3 relates, the influence of words proved not so good. The serpent convinces the woman that God does not want her and the man to eat from the tree in the center of the Garden because he wants to keep them from being like himself. The serpent deceives Eve with his speech, but his deceit is effective only because she allows herself to be convinced. She is so convinced that she has little trouble persuading the man to follow the serpent's lead as well.

When God finds the man hiding from him in the Garden and hears him speak of nakedness, he knows that the man and woman have broken the only rule he gave them. In fact, the man lies when he says he is naked, for Genesis 3:7 has told us that he and Eve have already made coverings for themselves. The truth is, Adam is ashamed of his sin but is afraid to say it. When God confronts him with his disobedience, he tells God it was Eve's fault—but ultimately God's fault for giving her to him. The woman, for her part, accuses the serpent. God dictates that they are all responsible for their own sin and punishes each one.

In this very first episode in human history, the Bible reveals that we have moved a long way from the power of words to produce good. In the mouths of people, words come to be used for harm. With the deceitfulness of the serpent, and the denial and finger-pointing of Adam and Eve, humankind is launched into life estranged from God. A little truth and honesty might have made the difference.

Speech is powerful, but its results can be wonderful or horrible. Proverbs 18:21 captures this reality when it says, "The tongue has the power of life and death, and those who love it will eat its fruit." The second part of this verse sounds puzzling but seems to be instructing us to be prepared to accept the consequences of what we say. Today we speak of a person "eating his words" in the sense of being forced to back down from something he said that has been proved wrong or inappropriate. In the proverb, this idea is broadened to refer to everything we say, harmful or helpful, right or wrong, good or bad. Our speech has effects, and we must live with them. We hope that most of what we say will be good, tasty "fruit," like strawberries, bananas and oranges. However, we must also swallow the bad, bitter "fruit" that tastes like lemons, crab apples or sour grapes.

Jewish rabbis tell a poignant story that drives home the point of Proverbs 18:21. As the story goes, Rabbi Simeon ben Gamaliel one day asked his servant to go and buy some good food for him in the market. When the servant returned home, he presented the rabbi with a tongue.

The next day, the rabbi told the servant to go to the market and buy some bad food. Again, the servant returned with a tongue.

When the rabbi asked the servant why he returned with a tongue both times, the servant made this astute observation: "Good comes from it and bad comes from it. When the tongue is good there is nothing better and when it is bad there is nothing worse."[1]

Five versions of this same story appear in Greek literature.[2] So the Bible shows us that the words we speak are capable of enormous good as well as disastrous evil, but the idea is really crosscultural. It's universal, as you and I know from our own experience. Our coworker can bring us to tears by harsh criticism of our performance, while moments later one positive note from our boss restores us to even greater achievement.

The ancients not only describe the tongue's enormous capacity to be good and bad but also recognize the utter control my tongue has over me and your tongue has over you. The tongue's power, like that of a South American dictator, does not come from brute strength but from craftiness and ruthlessness. Sirach, a second-century B.C. compilation of proverbial wisdom, describes the tongue as "the absolute master" (37:18).

A rabbinic midrash on Psalm 39:2 tells of a man who has a dream in which the feet, the hands, the eyes and the heart deride the tongue for boasting of its importance, even though each of them had just boasted of its own. Vindictively, the tongue vows to them that they will acknowledge its supremacy over them that very day. Later, as the king is passing by, the tongue fiendishly shouts out a crude remark. Unless the tongue apologizes, the man will be executed that very day. However, the tongue withholds its apology until the feet, the hands, the eyes and the heart offer their subordination.

The observations of the ancients remain true. Our tongues put our bodies in jeopardy time and time again. As children, we were spanked or put in "time out" for sassing our parents. We may have gotten in fights for put-downs we made to others. As adults, we still struggle with our tongue's iron grip over us. As Christians, we need to see this as an ongoing spiritual problem for which for which the Bible offers help. The tongue is strong, but God working in us is stronger.

Words as Drugs

Ancients sometimes capture the power of words by depicting words as medicinal drugs. Menander, a fourth-century B.C. Greek dramatist and philosopher, describes the beneficial role of words in this way: "The spoken word is man's physician in grief. For this alone has soothing claims for the soul. And the wisest men of times long ago call this a dainty drug."[3] The word *dainty* here does not mean weak and fragile; it refers to something that is good within its kind. Thus, as with any drug, when the right dosage is administered, words are an excellent aid to healing.

We know this to be true from our experience. When we are down emotionally and spiritually, the right words from the right person can turn us around. "It'll be OK" from my wife can work wonders for my mood. The power of words is not limited to emotional and spiritual realms, though. Words can also be balm for our physical ills. Why do we visit friends and loved ones in the hospital? Don't we go to encourage them to get better? And they usually do. Increasingly, doctors are acknowledging the critical difference that support from friends and family can make in a patient's recovery. The right words from the right people can put a person in the proper state of mind to promote the body's healing.

The right words not only affect people who are hospitalized. They can also prompt people to do such healthful things for their bodies as lose weight, stop smoking, lower their cholesterol and even fasten their seat belts.

Drugs don't always heal. Things can go wrong. Gorgias, a fourth-century B.C. Greek expert in rhetoric, cites both the positive and the negative potential of drugs to explain the power of words. He says that like drugs, words can "bring to an end either the disease or the life."[4] He adds that words can cause grief or pleasure or even fear; they can "drug or bewitch the soul." Proverbs 12:18 puts it like this: "Reckless words pierce like a sword, but the tongue of the wise brings healing."

Words can really help in many situations, but the wrong words at the wrong time can be extremely harmful. One wrong word, and the potential suicide victim follows through. On a day when a teenage girl feels good about herself, she may glow with joy when her dad tells her she is pretty, but on a moody day she may burst into angry tears at the very same words because they seem patronizing. A spouse's comment about the food or the house can initiate a big argument. An insecure husband can respond with physical abuse to his wife's remark about his job.

Recklessly harmful words can result from a speaker's own thoughtlessness; to a certain extent, however, they are a matter of perception. The adolescent teenage girl may perceive that her father's comment is patronizing. He may know it wasn't, but persuading her of his good motive is another matter. The resolution to many arguments involves people coming to grips with the intentions of their words. So one party explains, "I didn't mean it that way; I meant it this way." And the other party says, "I heard it this way, but if you meant it that way, I don't have a problem." Words cause the hurt; words bring about the healing.

Unlike Proverbs 12:18, Gorgias's remarks aren't about careless words so much as the negative effect of intentional words. He was a master of rhetoric. He knew that carefully crafted words can cause immense harm. A young boy can be persuaded by his peers to steal, to fight, to cheat, to lie to his parents. He can be coaxed into drug dealing and gang activity. He can be taught to hate one ethnic group or another. A teenage girl can be shamed or charmed into losing her virginity. Advertising can lure us into eating, drinking, smoking and buying things that are life-threatening. If we choose to, we can devastate someone by spreading false stories about them or embarrassing them in front of others.

When one of our sons was in first grade, he had an unbelievably devastating experience along these lines. My wife and I first picked up on it when we noticed that all of a sudden he wouldn't wear what used to be his favorite shorts to school. Then it was a pair of sneakers. Next it was his favorite Chicago White Sox cap, which I had purchased for him. Finally he wouldn't wear the red jacket given to him by his teenage cousin, whom he idolizes.

After questioning him, we learned that every day a sixth-grader at the bus stop chose something our son was wearing to make fun of in front of everyone. This had been going on for about three weeks. Our son had not done anything to trigger the ridicule. He was simply an easy target for the older boy, who felt a need to cut others down to alleviate his own low self-image.

Whether with the new-kid-on-the-block syndrome or a game of one-upmanship, we manage to find ways to hurt one another with our words even as adults. We know words are powerful. We continue to hurt and be hurt by them. As Christians, we are called to do better. The words of the Bible call for transformation of our speech.

When the rabbis adopted the drug analogy to convey the power of words, they were thinking more of the words of God's law, the Torah, than words people speak. They say that the Torah has "the power of life and death."[5] One rabbi adds, "For those who turn to the right in it, it is a drug of life; for those who turn to the left, it is a drug of death." Left represents disobedience, right represents obedience. The rabbis affirmed that the power to infuse a person's life with meaning, purpose and a future lay in the words of God's law.

Again, the analogy of a drug is appropriate. If one takes the drug (follows the law) as prescribed, abundant life results. If one does not take the drug, or perhaps has an allergic reaction to it (ignores or is disobedient to the law), one's life will be sick (judgment from God will result).

The Power of God's Words

In conceiving of the Torah as a life-or-death drug, the rabbis convey a truth that applies to the Bible as a whole and to the words of God that are contained in it. I have already noted the power of God's words to create the world and all the life in it. This is also emphasized in Psalm 33:6: "By the word of the LORD were the heavens made, their starry host by the breath of his mouth." Verse 8 points out that knowing the power of God's word to create should cause us to deeply respect God's authority over all things, including human affairs. The psalm continues:

For he spoke, and it came to be;
    he commanded, and it stood firm.

The LORD foils the plans of the nations;

> he thwarts the purposes of the peoples.

But the plans of the LORD stand firm forever,

> the purposes of his heart through all generations. (vv. 9-11)

The psalm goes on to draw the conclusion that what happens in the world continues to happen by the force of God's word. A king's success in battle does not stem from the size of his army or from the strength of his forces. It comes from God's decision. By the same word that began the universe, the Lord continues to mold and create this world into the shape he desires.

This means that God's word affects our lives whether we read the Bible and go to church or not. His word is heard in world affairs. It is present in our personal affairs. In no corner of the globe can we circumvent the power of God's word on us. We cannot hide in a dark cave or in a deserted wasteland. We can dive to the bottom of the deepest ocean or launch ourselves to the most distant star, and God's word is still there.

God's words extend from himself. They manifest his power and his desires, and they do this perfectly. Nothing of his will is lost in his words. They represent him exactly. Like him, then, God's words are invincible. Nothing can impede them from accomplishing what God wants.

Isaiah 55:10 compares God's word to rain. Rain always fulfills its purpose of producing flowers, crops and basic nourishment for us. In nature's cycle rain does return to the atmosphere in various forms, but not without doing what is supposed to do first. Verse 11 draws the comparison to God's word:

So is my word that goes forth from my mouth:

> It will not return to me empty,

but will accomplish what I desire

> and achieve the purpose for which I sent it.

The best way to get along in this world, then, is to recognize God's word in the world and to work along with it, just as we capitalize on rain to enhance our lives. Certainly, knowing God's word from the Bible will help us identify God's word in the swirl of life and the events of our times. God created us with a desire for his word. Growth in our spirituality will intensify this desire to the point where we crave God's word every day. We become like Jeremiah, who says that he relished eating God's words because they gave him so much joy (15:16). Consuming God's word can satisfy us like nothing else.

God's word is a powerful medicine for our good. However, every drug can have negative side effects. Rejection of God's word or failure to seek God's word opens up its invincible might against us. As if trying to swim against the tide, we will be swept away and crash on the rocks.

Just as God spoke the world into existence, so he can also speak its destruction. Genesis 6 says that at one point people became so evil that God was sorry he made them and determined to destroy everything on earth. Except for Noah's family and representative animals he saved to restock the world, God's word brought a flood that wiped out everything and everyone.

In Genesis 11, when people built a tower to celebrate and augment their own power and the power of their speech, God's word scattered them across the globe. In Genesis 19, God's word brought fire and brimstone down on the wicked people of Sodom and Gomorrah. In Exodus 14, God's word unleased death on the firstborn children of the Egyptians who had attempted to block his purposes for the Israelites. As the drama of Hebrew history plays out in the Old Testament, we read of Israel's enemies being crushed in battle by God's word, but also of Israel itself being carried off into captivity because its people no longer followed God's word.

Amos 1:2 characterizes God's voice as roaring from Zion and thundering from Jerusalem as God's punishments on Israel's neighbors are listed. God's word, Amos says, will cause fire to destroy the house of Hazael, the walls of Edom, of Gaza, of Tyre, of Rabbah, of Moab. God, by his word, will destroy the king of the Valley of Aven, the one who holds the scepter in Ashkelon, and the ruler and all the officials of Moab. In Jeremiah 5:14, because the people of Israel "have lied about the LORD" (v. 12), not believing his prophecy of destruction and famine for their rebelliousness, God says to Jeremiah, "I will make my words in your mouth a fire and these people the wood it consumes." As a warning against heeding self-proclaimed prophets who speak their own soothing words as if they were God's, Jeremiah 23:29 says, " 'Is not my word like fire,' declares the LORD, 'and like a hammer that breaks a rock in pieces?' "

God's word, then, cannot be stopped, bent or tossed away. It is power undeterred and in perpetual propulsion. To stand in its way is to be destroyed. To ride along with it is to be victorious in life. It's really that simple.

But we need to be careful not to make God out to be some impersonal force that has no personal compassion for humanity, or to somehow treat his words as though they were separate from himself. His words are an extension of himself which he can redirect, alter or even void if he so chooses. If this is not so, prayer is pointless and grace is meaningless. God's own will controls his words.

Jesus, God's Most Powerful Word

As powerful as God's word appears in the mouths of the Old Testament prophets, when we come to Jesus and the New Testament we enter another realm. In Jesus we see the personality of God's words come to life on the human plane in a way never imagined. "The Word became flesh and made his dwelling among us," declares John 1:14, and John 1:18 states that "the One and Only, who is at the Father's side, has made him known." In him resides the variability, compassion and determination of God's word. As John 1:17 says, "For the law was given through Moses; grace and truth came through Jesus Christ."

With choice wording, John's first verse flips our minds back to Genesis 1. John intertwines the word he is introducing with the words of God that produced the universe. He says the Word was present at creation and in verse 3 spells out that it was involved in creation. He wants us to see that this Word from God who became a man truly speaks the words of life (v. 4). By eating from the tree of the knowledge of good and evil and being cast out of the Garden (Gen 3), Adam and Eve caused us to lose access to the tree of life as well. But that path to life is reopened in Jesus. Those who believe in him, John 1:12 says, can become children of God. They are put on a new spiritual road to God.

But this is only because they believe Jesus does embody God's word, that in his actions and his words he speaks to us for God. John says that he and others have seen and heard Jesus and are positive that this is true.

Despite this, not everyone recognizes that Jesus is God's Word, just as not everyone recognized God's true prophets in the Old Testament. Some who recognize him even dare to oppose him. They cannot find the new path to life. Lost, they walk around in circles and die. This new Word of God named Jesus is the most powerful word of all, and we are foolish to ignore him or defy him.

One of the ways in which Jesus demonstrates that he is God's powerful Word is by performing miracles. The kind of power kindled at creation brings healing and life when Jesus utters simple words like "Be clean!" to a leper (Mt 8:3; Mk 1:41; Lk 5:13), "Come out!" to demons (Mt 8:16-17; Mk 1:23-28; 5:13; Lk 4:33-37; 8:32) and "Arise!" to the dead (Mt 9:18-26; Mk 5:38-43; Lk 7:14; 8:49-56). With other words he heals the paralytic (Mt 9:1-8; Mk 2:1-12; Lk 17:26), the sightless (Mt 20:29-34; Mk 10:46-52; Lk 18:35-43), the speechless (Mk 7:34) and the lame (Jn 5:1-14). The wind and the sea are calmed at his rebuke (Mt 8:23-27; Mk 4:35-41; Lk 9:22-25).

Jesus' words are authoritative, eliciting eager commitment from some like Matthew, who responds immediately to the words "Follow me!" (Mt 9:9; Mk 2:13-14; Lk 5:27-28), and Peter, Andrew, James and John, who do the same (Mt 4:18-22; Mk 1:16-20). Even those who remain uncommitted recognize the authority inherent in his teaching (Mt 7:28-29; Mk 1:21-22; Lk 4:31-32). Jesus knew that the weight of his words, as the Word of God, would endure forever. In Luke 21:33 Jesus says, "Heaven and earth will pass away, but my words will never pass away." His words will not go away if we ignore them. They are always present, and they are always trying to get our attention. We are foolish not to heed them.

Jesus' words are life, as he says in John 6:63. This is so because *he* is life. He is the living water (Jn 4:13-14) and the bread of life (Jn 6:25-59). To eat and drink this new and final Word of God, to respond to his teaching, is the only way to eternal life available to us. What he teaches comes from the heart of God.

To challenge this truth would be like trying to swim upstream in rapids. We will be swept away to destruction. To contemporary skeptics who doubted the divine authority of his teaching, Jesus offered a guaranteed invitation that remains for us today in John 7:16-17: "My teaching is not my own. It comes from him who sent me. If anyone chooses to do God's will, he will find out whether my teaching comes from God or whether I speak on my own."

The power of Jesus' words comes from who he is. His voice is God's. His being is an extension of God. He is God's Word.

As the source of Jesus' word power is God, so the source of any word power his disciples might have is Jesus. He alone is our link to God's powerful word. When he sends his disciples out in his name, he gives them his authority to cast out demons and heal disease (Mt 10:1; Mk 6:7; Lk 9:1; 10:9). They were not to withhold this power but to share it liberally with those in need as a way of drawing people to Jesus (Mt 10:8). When the seventy return, Luke 10:17 records them as saying, "Lord, even the demons submit to us in your name." They know the power that poured out in their words was not theirs but came from him. Nevertheless, in Luke 10:20 Jesus warns them not to gloat but to rejoice in God's grace toward them.

He says this to remind them of what happened not long after the twelve came back from their earlier tour, as described in Mark 9:14-29 (also Mt 17:14-20; Lk 9:37-42). With Peter, James and John, Jesus came down from the mountain where the transfiguration had taken place. At the foot of the mountain, a crowd was squabbling with the disciples, who had been unsuccessful in casting a demon out of a man's son. The power of the disciples' words to heal and to cast out demons was gone. They were humiliated. Apparently they had begun to think that the power was theirs. In doing so, they cut themselves off from its source. One hopes that they never again forgot that the power in their words depended on Jesus, the Word of God.

The power of Jesus was with the disciples not only when they did miracles in his name but also when they were called on to testify for his name. Even though their lives might be threatened, they could count on the fact that his word would remain with them. In Luke 21:14-15 he tells them, "But make up your mind not to worry beforehand how you will defend yourselves. For I will give you words and wisdom that none of your adversaries will be able to resist or contradict."

After Jesus ascended to heaven, he left behind someone else who would continue to transmit his power to his disciples. Jesus introduces this person to his disciples as the Counselor (Jn 15:26), the Spirit of Truth (Jn 16:13) and the power from on high with which they will be clothed (Lk 23:49). Acts 2 describes how this Spirit descended on them and empowered them with both bold speech and mighty deeds. They confront authorities (Acts 4:1-21; 5:17-32; 23:1-11; 24-26). They speak to angry mobs (13:46-52; 17:1-9; 19:23-40; 22:1-21). They heal the lame (3:6-10), cast out demons (8:7; 16:18; 19:11) and raise the dead (20:7-12). They are even empowered with the means to transmit this Spirit to others. Acts 2:38 says that upon baptism in the name of Jesus, a person receives this same Holy Spirit. Direct access to the everlasting Word of God now is available to everyone.

The Spirit received by every new Christian provides the power for each of us to speak boldly the special word of God about Christ as the pioneers of faith did in Acts. The ability to preach the gospel comes from the power of the Spirit that Christ gives us. In 1 Thessalonians 1:5, Paul states, "Our gospel came to you not simply with words, but also with power, with the Holy Spirit and with deep conviction." Although Paul mentions three distinct items here, he seems to assume a dynamic association between the three, with power and conviction being dependent on the presence of the Holy Spirit. The point is that Paul recognizes that the special ability of his words to convince the Thessalonians to become Christians did not come from any natural rhetorical skills. The power of his words came from God through Christ and the Holy Spirit Christ gave him. His words were God's words, and as we discovered earlier, God's words always fulfill their purpose.

In Colossians 1:28-29, Paul tries to explain this dynamic that drives his life: "We proclaim him, admonishing and teaching everyone with all wisdom, so that we may present everyone perfect in Christ. To this end I labor, struggling with all his energy, which so powerfully works in me." Paul knows that a powerful force in his life makes him effective for Christ. This goes beyond the evangelistic proclamation of the gospel. It extends to his words of discipleship too. The word of God works in him to help people grow up into the best they can be for Christ.

For this Paul has help from God, beyond the power that God provides him. The growing dynamic of the word of God in the believer also is involved. First Peter 1:23 says, "For you have been born again, not of perishable seed, but of imperishable, through the living and enduring word of God." Peter then quotes Isaiah 40:6-8, which pictures a field in which God's word stands up under a hot sun, even though people wither like grass and flowers.

God's invincible word active in us can make us thrive despite the impediments life sets before us. God's word can turn the barren desert of our lives into a lush valley. A miraculous transformation takes place when the word of God works in us. We are taken out of a hopeless situation and born again into a life filled with meaning and hope. Like a seed, the word of God brings growth. Our life blossoms with the beauty that only God can bring. We can see that God's creation of the universe did not stop on the sixth day of Genesis 1—it continues in us.

This wonderful transformation of our lives, though, does not begin within ourselves. We have no power to effect a rebirth. The new seed must be planted in us. The word of God must come to us from someone else. And so Peter concludes verse 25, "And this is the word that was preached to you." This is the word that continues to be preached, continues its transformation of individuals, continues its expansion of the kingdom of God.

The power of God's word in the New Testament, then, centers on Jesus, the power of his words and those who preach his gospel. The power of the word comes from the creative word of God himself. It simply comes more powerfully but also more personally in Jesus and continues to spread from person to person through the dynamic of the Spirit.

The Origin of Word Power

Do you believe in magic words? Does *abracadabra* bring a rabbit out of a hat? Does *open sesame* move doors hiding treasure? Does *hocus-pocus* release magical forces? Perhaps as a child watching Dorothy click her ruby shoes and repeat, "There's no place like home," in *The Wizard of Oz,* you wondered. But what do you think now? And more important, what does the Bible reveal about magic words? Are there words that have power independent of their speaker, so that when we speak them they are activated? Where does the power of words come from, anyway?

Believe it or not, some scholars see evidence in the Old Testament that words have power of their own, quite separate from the speaker.[6] In other words, they believe in magical words, words that when spoken have power to manipulate events. Briefly examining some of the key passages these scholars cite will reveal this notion to be erroneous and misleading. The origin of word power has to do with the relationship of the speaker and the hearer, not the words alone. Thinking through this will help us better understand our relationship to the words we utter.

James Barr has exposed the failings of this view on two fronts.[7] I wish to focus on a third area that involves key Old Testament passages featuring blessings and curses.

Judges 17:1-4 tells us about a woman (from Ephraim) who, having discovered that eleven hundred shekels have been stolen from her, cursed the unknown thief. The thief turns out to be her son, Micah. He confesses his guilt and returns the money. Immediately, she offers a blessing on her son. Does she offer the blessing because she believes that she must counteract the words of the curse, as Walther Eichrodt concludes?[8] No; having heard her son's confession and received his payment of restitution, this woman simply calls on God to reevaluate her son in this light, saying, "The LORD bless you, my son." The power of her curse or her blessing resides not in the words themselves, but in God.

Leviticus 19:14 forbids cursing the deaf. Some speculate that this is because it amounts to using the independent power of words to unfair advantage over a defenseless, unhearing victim.[9] However, a recent, thorough study of curses in the Old Testament by H. C. Brichto concludes, "There is no evidence that an unjustified curse was regarded as efficacious, nor that curses had to be pronounced in the hearing of the victim."[10] The injunction against cursing someone who is deaf probably would apply to any kind of defamatory speech that would put the person down in front of others. Not hearing, the person would be unable to defend himself.

In 1 Samuel 14:24-48 Saul offers a general curse on anyone in his army who eats food that day. Unaware of the curse, his son Jonathan tastes some honey. After discovering that Jonathan has done this, Saul even offers a specific curse of death on him. Yet neither curse comes to pass; the army is victorious, and Jonathan lives. Apparently God judged Saul's curses to be out of order and did not consider them to stand up against his own desire to bless Jonathan's efforts that day (1 Sam 14:6-15). As Proverbs 26:2 sums it up, "Like a fluttering sparrow or a darting swallow, an undeserved curse does not come to rest."

Numbers 5:16-28 puts this principle to the ultimate test in a suggested court procedure for discovering whether a woman has committed adultery against her husband. Upon pronouncing a curse on herself, she consumes a bitter drink. If she is guilty, her abdomen will swell and her thigh will "waste away." Yet the text makes it very clear that God will not bring this judgment on her if she is innocent. Neither the words uttered nor the bitter drink will bring a punishment, but God.

Finally, we need to address confusion regarding Isaac's refusal to revoke the blessing Jacob received by trickery in Genesis 27:33-37 and to confer it on Esau, as he originally intended. Isaac could have revoked the blessing, but he viewed the successful trickery as providential. Thinking that God was behind it, Isaac deemed it pointless to revoke the blessing and confer it on Esau.

A curse, then, does not have a life of its own. A speaker can rescind it, as we have seen, but God can also choose to ignore it, since by its nature a curse or blessing requests that matters be placed in God's court of justice.

The idea that words have some kind of power or life that overrides normal communication between a speaker and a hearer does not have any biblical foundation. The origin of word power is not in words themselves. It begins with the one who utters the words but is consummated only when the hearer accepts the communication and is convinced. The relationship between speaker and hearer will affect whether the hearer accepts, rejects or ignores the communication.

Word power is not dependent on persuasiveness, however, because the speaker might have such authority over the hearer that convincing him or her is not necessary. A private in the army is supposed to obey without question. Good employees submit to their boss. We obey police officers. The power in such cases is not in words alone but in the people who speak them and their relationship to us.

Therefore, we are responsible when we hurt others by what we say. We cannot blame the words. They are extensions of ourselves. If we discover that we have been misunderstood, we can make corrections. When we say things we wish we hadn't, we can seek forgiveness by apologizing. When we are kicking ourselves for failing to say something we wish we'd said, we can return to the person and say it.

It's Up to You

In our exploration so far, we have found plenty of evidence for the power of words. We have seen that human words have the potential to hurt or to help. We have examined the power of God's words and God's Word. We have determined that the power of words has to do with the one who speaks and the one who receives.

Words belong to you and me. We can make them do what we want, good or bad. The choice is somewhere inside ourselves. Improving in our use of this God-given ability to speak is a spiritual journey. God's own words are perfectly tuned to his perfect nature. Our quest is to be more and more like him, within the limitations of our own human frailty and the evil in the world around us. As Christians, we have the resources of God to help us. Christ has given us the Holy Spirit.

The next two chapters will deal with those times when we sidestep the Holy Spirit within us and use the power of speech for harm.

2

Daily Speech Sins

Careless Hurt

*M*ost of us violate ethics of talk every day. We fill so much air with talk each day that we can hardly help saying something out of place or unfair to someone else. Our desire to be right, to get ahead, to gain control, to be heard, to defend ourselves, or simply our carelessness can prompt us to say all kinds of things at the expense of others. As Christians we regret saying these things and, let us hope, attempt to make amends. But even catching ourselves when we sin in our speech is tough. Self-monitoring our every word is impossible. Still, we all can do better.

The purpose of this chapter and the next is to help us know what to watch for. The Bible and other ancient writings clearly identify certain speech sins and condemn them. People have changed in many ways since Bible times, but the ways we hurt each other in our talk has not changed. Categorizing speech sins like this does not cut to the root of our sin, but it is a good place to start. We need to know what we are listening for as we try to improve the way we talk to the glory of God.

Sometimes we fail in our speech because, for whatever reasons, we just don't think about what we are saying. Irresponsibly, we say things that are insensitive, pass on gossip, put people down or just let our anger take over. These careless sins of speech will be discussed in this chapter.

Tactlessness

We often describe this failure in speech by saying that someone "put her foot in her mouth." Sometimes we just don't watch where we are going verbally and end up stepping on someone's feelings. We are insensitive. The joke or wisecrack might be funny in certain circumstances, but we misjudge or fail to assess the situation. The hurt may not even be a failing on our part. The person's bad reaction to what we say may be beyond our ability to anticipate. Regardless, though, our comment has made a bad situation worse. We have embarrassed someone, deflated an already bruised ego, detonated a rising anger or brought further damage to an ailing relationship. We obtusely thought that because we were happy, everyone was, or since we considered a joke funny, everyone wanted to hear it right then.

One of the best attempts to describe tactless speech is found in Proverbs 25:20:

Like one who takes away a garment on a cold day,
> or like vinegar poured on soda,
> is one who sings songs to a heavy heart.

The first line conjures up the image of a street person huddled in a dark corner on a wintry night. He lies shivering, with nothing but a dirty, unlined trench coat around him. Along comes a gang of kids with nothing better to do than cause trouble. So they grab his coat and run off with it, only to throw it in a trash can a few blocks down the way.

Our talk can be like that. We're bored and can't think of anything to do. So we say things to a friend just to get a rise out of him, or we pick on a little sister who can't tie her shoe. Maybe we say something sarcastic to a colleague at work who is struggling with a task. Verbally, we kick them when they are down.

The RSV (following the Septuagint) translates the second line "or like vinegar poured on a wound." In any case, the moral is about insensitive irritation. Vinegar on baking soda erupts with fizz. Vinegar in a wound produces searing pain. Both present images of anger bursting out in reaction to thoughtless comments.

What triggers this reaction in each of us may vary. I don't react well to my wife's criticisms of something I've written if she begins with a long list of problems before making positive comments. Maybe you are sensitive to comments about your clothes, your cooking, your weight or aspects of your job.

Perfectly suitable words can be perfectly unsuitable when spoken in the wrong setting. It is cruelly insensitive to sing gaily in the presence of someone who has just lost a loved one.[1] A friend who has just been dumped by her boyfriend doesn't need to hear us play a new love song on the stereo or have us tell about our great date the night before. What a sorrowing friend needs is words that are fitting, words that bring comfort and hope, music that builds confidence and faith. Maybe she needs our silent understanding.

The first-century A.D. Greek moralist Plutarch is right when he observes, "There are times when we are more aroused by jokes than by insults," and "The man who cannot engage in joking at a suitable time, discreetly and skillfully, must avoid jokes altogether."[2] Good-natured joking between friends is great fun. However, without good timing and sensitivity, ribbing can cut like a knife. A good friend will hold the smart comment or the funny joke until it can be enjoyed as intended.

For those of us who have ever been aroused on a sleepy Saturday morning by a parent, spouse or roommate's flinging open the drapes and chirping about what a beautiful day it is, the wisdom of Proverbs 27:14 will resonate: "If a man loudly blesses his neighbor early in the morning, it will be taken as a curse."

Situations into which we can inject tactless speech are innumerable. We all know what it is like to be offended by someone's tactless comment.

Perhaps those painful moments can help us be more sensitive in our speech toward others. Epictetus, a first-century Stoic philosopher, offers advice that we still need to hear: "We must remember what is the proper time for song . . . for play . . . when to jest . . . when to laugh."[3]

Included in tactless speech is what could be called *tacky* speech. Sometimes what we say doesn't harm someone personally but sullies the social environment generally. Rather than being insensitive to a person, we are oblivious to social standards. We fail in verbal etiquette, perhaps with poor grammar, speaking when we should be quiet or interrupting someone who is speaking. Regardless, our speech damages the occasion and draws negative attention to us. Vice President Dan Quayle was an easy target for criticism in this area, from his misspelling of *potato* in a New York classroom to his poor grammar in denouncing the *Murphy Brown* television show.

Aristotle can help us in our thinking about this area of speech ethics. He observes that in ethical behavior there is always a "mean," or middle, between two extremes.[4] The middle is what we strive for. It is virtuous or good behavior. The extremes we seek to avoid. One of the three virtues of speech that Aristotle outlines is to be ready-witted. People should aim to be engaging and positive in what they say. The excess extreme he calls buffoonery—tactless speech. The extreme deficiency he calls boorishness—what I have called tacky speech. Included in boorishness is socially unacceptable speech, ranging from using the wrong words to introduce oneself to the queen to telling sexually explicit jokes in front of children. It includes all kinds of vulgarity and lewdness, using the Lord's name in vain and the many expletives that people employ without thinking.

One day when my son Kyle was eight and we were walking out the front door together, he was treated to the pungent sounds of cursing as a tradesman on a ladder four doors away struggled with a piece of guttering he was trying to install. The man could be heard all the way down the block and was oblivious to his surroundings.

Flippant joking about sex is common on television sitcoms, in schools and in health-club locker rooms. The Jewish Talmud, however, rightly instructs people to leave what is private and intimate out of the public arena of conversation: "All know for what purpose a bride enters the bridal canopy, yet whoever speaks obscenely of it, even if a sentence of seventy years of happiness had been sealed for him, it is reversed for evil."[5]

The Talmud even has good advice for those of us who read Scripture publicly, suggesting that when readers come across indelicate expressions regarding things like sexuality, they substitute wording that is more polite.[6] Finally, Rabbi Ishmael states the general advice for us plainly: "One should always discourse in decent language."[7]

Many lists of sins for Christians to avoid appear in the New Testament. Ephesians 5:3-4 concludes by naming three sins of speech, all of which fall into this category of tacky speech: "obscenity," "foolish talk" and "coarse joking." All three are said to be "out of place," and thanksgiving is suggested as a more beneficial use of speech. These three sins are listed only here in the New Testament.

The first word usually is employed to convey an attitude that is ugly or wicked. It is related to another word, used in Colossians 3:8, which more specifically refers to foul, obscene speech. The root word on which both are based carries with it a sense of shame. Speaking in this manner should cause us shame. It is socially unacceptable.

The second term, "foolish talk," has more to do with silliness. Sometimes, in idle moments, we kid one another. Often this is fun. But sometimes the kidding turns sour when someone takes something the wrong way.

The third term, "coarse joking," can actually convey either of two extremes, depending on context. In a context that presumes the positive, the word means "witty" and describes people with the "gift of gab." I think of radio talk-show hosts, comedians and many public speakers. These people command our attention because they blend wit, charm and warmth with occasional insight. But we all know that such skills can be combined with crudity and grossness to produce "trash radio," gutter comedy and incitement to riot. This is what the word means in the negative context of Ephesians 5:4. Coarse joking is using the gift of gab to talk down and dirty. This is a perversion of speech and is rightly condemned.

Tactless speech, then, basically is mindless. Its harmfulness basically depends on the personal or social context in which it is uttered. We speak this way when we don't know or don't care what other people think or feel. Sensitivity to people's feelings is an ethical basic for Christians. We need to work hard to stand above the crowd in this area.

Gossip

Children know there is something wrong about breaking the unspoken trust within their ranks. A child who regularly breaks trust over trivial problems that could be resolved within the group is branded with a special name, "tattletale." As parents, we sometimes appreciate the tattletale who informs us of the sins of our children so that we can discipline them. On the other hand, we also know that the tattletale is generating a bad habit that endangers not only their childhood friendships but their later adult relationships too. Talking about other people behind their backs is dangerous business. Even though, as in tactless speech, there may be no intent to hurt others, the potential for harm is enormous.

Gossip strikes at the very heart of human relationships. It occurs when we would rather talk *about* someone than *to* them. We are more interested in impressing people with our knowledge of the news than in ascertaining its factuality or how the subject of our news will be affected. When the personal chauffeur of a media personality writes a revealing book, even if we are interested, we know that something about this is probably unfair to the celebrity. An entire journalistic industry of magazines, columns and so-called newspapers does nothing but publish secrets about the stars. At the personal level, we feel for these stars, even if we don't like them, because we know how we would feel if our friends and neighbors talked about us like that.

Proverbs observes that gossip creates problems for friendship. Proverbs 11:13 says that "a gossip betrays a confidence," and 16:28 says that "a gossip separates close friends." Proverbs 20:19 warns against friendship with someone "who talks too much." The problem is *betrayal*. Gossip severs the trust that undergirds friendship. If the gossip gets back around to the subject, she knows that someone has betrayed her. When she discovers who initiated the news, you can bet that any friendship will be over.

Plutarch pictures gossip as fire and mentions situations where gossips have brought down entire cities.[8] Because of this he brands gossips with one of the worst social stigmas. He calls them traitors, and he's right. Just as a Benedict Arnold or a Julius Rosenberg[9] disregards loyalty to his fellow citizens and his government for personal gain, so do gossips undermine the trust of friendship in order to have a few moments in the spotlight as they share their secrets.

We may think that Plutarch exaggerated, but still today governments are brought down by information, true or false, that becomes public through gossip. Washington, D.C., is plagued by "leaks" to the press; such leaks opened up the fiascos of Watergate, the Iran-Contra affair and the public circus of the judicial hearings to confirm Clarence Thomas's appointment to the Supreme Court.

The party game called Telephone, in which a simple message is whispered down the line, only to find how much it has changed by the time it reaches the last person, readily illustrates another problem with gossip: even if the information being spread begins as true, it won't take many links in the chain before it is distorted. Plutarch conveys the degenerative property of gossip with a comparison from agriculture: "For as wheat shut up in a jar is found to have increased in quantity but to have deteriorated in quality, likewise when a story finds its way to a chatterer, it generates a large addition of falsehood and thereby destroys its credit."[10]

When we hear gossip, we usually don't know where in the chain we are. Therefore, we should assume what we are hearing is a distortion of the truth. We should distrust what we are hearing and, if appropriate, check with the person who is the subject of the gossip. Mindlessly repeating what we have heard adds yet another link of betrayal against that person.

We also need to take care that we are not the unwitting instruments of gossip. Ecclesiastes 10:20 warns us to be careful whom we are with when we talk about others, "because a bird of the air may carry your words, and a bird on the wing may report what you say." In other words, gossip travels fast, and we never know for sure that someone nearby won't pass on what we said about someone else. The person we are talking to may not like the friend we are talking about and may be only too glad to twist what we have said into gossip. We may be sharing a prayer concern; they may be spreading gossip.

Unfortunately, too many of us act like starving animals slopping up "the words of a gossip . . . like choice morsels," as Proverbs 18:8 and 26:22 state. Jewish midrash paints an even more vivid picture of gossips before it draws us up short: "If one dog barks, all others gather round and bark also for no purpose, but you must not be so, for you are holy."[11]

You and I are people made in the image of God. We are not dogs, and we shouldn't act like them. For people devoted to God, gossiping is all too unbecoming. Rather, let's heed the sound advice in Sirach: "Cherish your friend, keep faith with him," and "Never repeat gossip!" When we hear gossip, we may need to follow another of Sirach's healthy prescriptions: "Admonish your friend—he may not have done it; and if he did, that he may not do it again. Admonish your neighbor—he may not have said it; and if he did, that he may not say it again. Admonish your friend—often it may be slander; every story you must not believe."[12]

The word *gossip* often conjures up images of women talking over their backyard fences as they hang out their laundry, in a neighborhood kaffee-klatsch or on the telephone. Such a caricature of women as gossips goes back a long way. In the Jewish Talmud (*Kiddah* 49b), a rabbi teaches that while ten portions of gossip descended to the world at its inception, nine of these portions were taken by women. *Pirqe Abot,* one of the earliest sources of rabbinic wisdom, in 1:5 warns its readers, "Don't talk too much with women!"

Plutarch tells a story with a plot that could have played on *I Love Lucy* or *The Dick Van Dyke Show.*[13] It seems the wife of a Roman senator was pestering her husband to tell her about a secret debate that had been occurring the last few days. Desiring to demonstrate to his wife that she could not keep a secret, the senator told her they were discussing what to do about the report that a lark had been seen flying around with a golden helmet and a spear. After telling her this, he began his walk to the Forum. As soon as he left the house, she told her young maid the news but added "that refrain common to every babbler, 'Keep this quiet and tell it to no one!' " Well, the maid told another servant, who told it to her boyfriend who

. . . By the time the senator was taking his place at the Forum, a colleague approached with some urgent news: "A lark has been seen flying around with a golden helmet and a spear and the senate is going to decide what to do about it today." The senator laughed and spoke as if to his wife: "All praise to your speed, my wife!"

In the New Testament, the Pastoral Epistles' warnings against gossip are directed specifically at women. First Timothy 5:13 takes aim at young widows (presumably those under age sixty, judging from 1 Timothy 5:9). The apostle does not want financial aid going to them because, he says, "they get into the habit of being idle and going about from house to house. And not only do they become idlers, but also gossips and busybodies, saying things they ought not to."

Actually, the word translated "gossips" is used only here in the New Testament. Other passages in the Pastorals use a word more associated with slander than with gossip. First Timothy 3:11 notes that deacons' wives (or female deacons) should not be, as the NIV translates the word, "malicious talkers." In Titus 2:3 the same word, translated "slanderers," depicts unacceptable behavior for "older" Christian women.

Whether gossip is really more of a problem for women is difficult to say. Probably wherever decision-making power lies solely in the hands of men, as is the case in many churches, women will be tempted to find out what's going on around the fringes. Christian women must resist this temptation, which so often leads to disaster. Also, Christian women must realize that breaking down this unbecoming gender stereotype requires superior effort on their part. This is crucial for any woman who desires to respond to the growing opportunities for leadership inside and outside the church.

Images of men gossiping persist, too. Even in ancient Greece, men were said to gossip in the barbershop. Plutarch notices, "It is not strange that barbers are a talkative clan, for the greatest chatterboxes stream in and sit in their chairs, so that they are themselves infected with the habit."[14] At the barbershop, the gas station, the office and the church foyer, men will gossip about sports, debating the prowess of Rickey Henderson or Steve Young, or second-guessing the decisions of the coach or manager in last night's game. No doubt, the Stoic philosopher Epictetus was aiming at men when he urged his first-century followers not to waste their time talking about "gladiators, horse-races, or athletes."[15]

Gossip is a problem for all of us, men and women. It is a problem in the church and in the general population. People love to talk about other people, their problems, their misfortunes, their plans, their secrets. As Christians, we must strive to restrain ourselves. We must think carefully about whether information we have should be shared. We must encourage people to check their facts. We must confront gossips with their mischief.

Mockery

Some of the ugliest-sounding words in the English language have been coined by groups of people who want to ridicule other groups. Sinister distortions of racial names spoken in haughty and degrading tones—*nigger, kike, gook, chink, polack* and *spic*—symbolize centuries of hatred for no other reason than the fact that differences of custom and physical development have formed distinct groups of people who act and look different from one another.

Of course, mockery is not just racial slurs. Mockery can be directed at anyone who is weak or has encountered misfortune. The mocker feels superior. He believes his victim incapable of fending off his taunts and insults. He feels that the majority of those around him agree with his point of view, or at least that no one will try to stop him. He feels power. In the end, mockery is a power play to feed a threatened ego, either racially or individually.

So many images of mockery flood our experience. Black American slaves were trained to look at the ground and say, "Yessuh, boss!" The mentally ill are verbally tortured by misunderstanding families. The physically handicapped must deal with the stares and laughter of insensitive people. Students with learning disabilities hear their classmates call them "dumb."

The fact is that anyone can be mocked for anything. All of us bear the psychologically devastating scars of ridicule. Short, tall, skinny, fat, plain, smart, dumb, slow—we found as children that our playmates made quick work of discovering our "deficiencies" and exploiting them to our faces. Our nose, our hair, our names (especially middle), our bike, our house, our father's occupation were all available for ridicule.

I recall slugging my next-door neighbor in the stomach on the way home from school because she was ridiculing my father's occupation with the post office. Such incidents remain vivid for all of us. Terms like *nerd, jock, Jewish Princess, wimp* and *redneck* still resonate in junior-high and high-school hallways—or have been replaced by new ways of putting down people's distinctive interests and personalities.

We are all subject to mockery, even though the brunt falls on those less fortunate. If someone wants to find something about us to make fun of, they can, simply because everyone of us is different in some way. Once I overheard a neighbor child mocking my child's name, Gavin, simply because he had never heard it before. I've heard children say that no one can play if they have a certain letter in their name. Adults may be more subtle, but similar antics take place at work and in our associations with others. Wisecracks about people's weight, clothes, race and gender are heard daily in office conclaves. Recently, after a heavyset woman was hired in a certain company, someone commented that if the company was not careful, the weight on that side of the building would tip it over.

Psalm 10:9-10 pictures the mocker as an animal seeking its prey:

He lies in wait like a lion in cover;

he lies in wait to catch the helpless;

he catches the helpless and drags them off in his net.

His victims are crushed, they collapse;

they fall under his strength.

He says to himself, "God has forgotten;

he covers his face and never sees."

Of course we are not animals. The victims of mockery carry emotional and psychological scars with them. God has created us with an ability to be sensitive to others that we must use. Yet mockery has always been a problem for us. Even ancient writers tried to defend easy victims of mockery. A very old Egyptian writing instructs:

Do not jeer at a blind man nor tease a dwarf;

neither interfere with the condition of a cripple.

Do not taunt a man who is in the hand of God,

nor scowl at him if he errs. . . .

Do not reproach someone older than you,

for he has seen the Sun before you.[16]

Proverbs 14:31 and 17:5 mention the poor as potential objects of mockery. Sirach names the poor (10:22), the old (8:6), the "embittered" (7:11), the "repentant sinner" (8:5) and even the drunk (31:31). Hesiod, one of the most ancient of Greek poets, tries to safeguard orphans and aged fathers from mockery.[17] Aristophanes criticizes the common practice of employing verbal abuse of slaves for humor in Greek drama.[18] Until recently the same criticism would apply to the treatment of blacks and members of other minorities in American literature (like Mark Twain's Jim in *Huckleberry Finn*) and radio and film *(Amos 'n' Andy)*.

When we are tempted to ridicule someone, it is wise to remember what Isocrates says: "Taunt no man for his misfortune, for fate is common to all and the future is a thing unseen."[19] We ourselves will become old, perhaps handicapped. Financial disaster could make us poor. Someday we could be the member of a racial minority. We could be become overweight. We must think how we would feel if we were the target of the verbal abuse we are about to dish out.

Although mockers think that the weaker person they berate is defenseless and abandoned by God, they are quite wrong. God views the action of the mocker as an insult to his creation and to himself personally. Not only do mockers have little regard for others, but they are so full of themselves that they don't think much of God either. Psalm 10:4 observes, "In all [the wicked man's] thoughts there is no room for God." Psalm 12:5 promises that God will hear the cries of the oppressed and arise to avenge them. Proverbs 17:5 warns, "He who mocks the poor shows contempt for their Maker; whoever gloats over disaster will not go unpunished."[20]

Instances of mockery are numerous in biblical history. Peninnah goads Hannah to the point of tears over her barrenness (1 Sam 1:7). Ishmael mocks Isaac (Gen 21:9). Job complains that he is being mocked by young men (Job 30). David appeals to God, complaining that he has felt the ridicule of his enemies as they gloat over his misfortune, saying, "Aha! Aha!" (Ps 35:21; 40:15). Young teens make fun of Elisha's balding head (2 Kings 2:23).

Jeremiah (20:8) complains to God that his obedient prophecies of destruction have brought him "insult and reproach all day long." Philo of Alexandria, a first-century Jew who tried to interpret Jewish thought in a Greek mindset, points out that Jews as a people were a common subject of ridicule by Greeks and members of other nationalities.[21]

Like the Jews, early Christian believers came to expect ridicule from their pagan neighbors and friends because of their faith commitment, but they also were ridiculed by jealous Jews who viewed the spread of Christianity as a threat. On Paul and Barnabas's very first missionary journey, they met this kind of resistance in Pisidian Antioch. Because of the interest in the gospel being generated within the Jewish community, Acts 13:45 says that some Jews publicly "talked abusively against what Paul was saying." To the Thessalonians Paul confides that in Philippi "we had previously suffered and been insulted" (1 Thess 2:2).

Early Christians were easy fodder for those who wished to mock them, because what they believed seemed so far-fetched. The idea of God's becoming fully a human being seemed ridiculous both to Jew and to Greek. But the further thought that this God-man succumbed to the cruelest form of execution known to humankind was beyond comprehension for most. The cross was for slaves and robbers, certainly not a so-called god. What kind of god, they thought, would undergo such indignity and humiliation? If he was a god, he must have been exceedingly foolish and weak. Only foolish and weak people would worship someone like this.

Paul, in fact, openly admits in 1 Corinthians 1:18 that "the message of the cross is foolishness" according to human wisdom. However, Paul views its "foolishness" as its strength. It goes far beyond what is humanly imaginable. It's so fantastic, it must be true. What mere human could even make this up?

Paul realizes that the power of the cross lies in what Christ endured on our behalf. Jesus curtailed his power and submitted to the utmost pain and indignity because he loves us. His power is seen in his abandonment of power to die in our place. The power of the cross erupts in the resurrection and the new life it makes possible for everyone who believes.

Jesus' conduct on the cross became a model for early Christians, as it still should be for us today. He was mocked (Mt 27:27-31, 41, 44; Lk 22:63-65), as he had warned his followers he would be (Mt 20:19; Mk 1:34; Lk 18:32). The guards blindfolded him, then slapped him and asked him to prophesy who struck him. They fashioned a crown from a thorny vine and played a scurrilous form of make-believe, taunting him for the claims he made. The priests, teachers and elders of the Jews laughed with glee that this one who said he had the power of God was helpless to prevent his death. Even the robbers being crucified with him joined in the jeering. But he said nothing; he did nothing; he accepted the abuse, confident that he would be vindicated and that his suffering would clear away a new path to God for you and me.

First Peter 2:21-24 teaches that this is what we should do when we are ridiculed, whether for our faith or for our oversized nose. We must take it like Jesus did, putting our trust in God and believing earnestly that he will put things right. We can believe that greater good can come from our lack of retaliation than from our natural urge to respond in kind to those who harass us. We are not to repay "insult with insult, but with blessing, because to this you were called so that you may inherit a blessing" (1 Pet 3:9). We are to "bless those who curse" us, as Christ directed (Lk 6:28; Rom 12:14; 1 Cor 4:12).[22]

So we should bear insult and ridicule with a spiritual fortitude like that of Christ. But we ourselves must keep from using our speech to disparage someone else. As the rabbis wisely advise, "Despise no man!" and "Judge everyone with the scales weighted in his favor."[23]

Hot-Tempered Speech

A motorist cuts us off, threatening our safety. Our boss tells us to redo some work we had painstakingly put together. Our neighbor acts as if her son is perfect and our son is completely at fault. We become sick and have to cancel our long-planned trip to Hawaii. We burn the dinner. The umpire calls our daughter out at third base. Our child knocks over the lamp and lies about it. Someone makes fun of our handicap.

These are common scenarios for anger to emerge in us. But not everyone would get angry in these situations. Some of us would, and some of us wouldn't. We might not even get angry every time any of these things happen. When we are in a certain mood, we might ignore the careless motorist or laugh at burning the pot roast. Sometimes being tired or tense can make little things trigger anger in us. High blood pressure can make someone prone to anger. Many different causes and situations, then, bring on anger in people. Yet we all get angry sometimes.

What happens when we become angry? We experience an emotional surge that inevitably seeks a physical outlet. Often we say things we regret. We curse the motorist. We walk away muttering about the ignorance of our boss and throw our project in the trash bin. We tell the neighbor off. We pound on the bed and cry at missing our trip. We swear at the pot roast or the kids for distracting us. We yell at the umpire. We scream at our clumsy, irresponsible child. We complain to God about our handicap.

Anger may find its way out in other ways than through our mouths. We may take some action like honking our horn or tailgating the thoughtless motorist or spanking our child. We may say or do nothing, internalize our anger and develop a headache, or worse, an ulcer. However, hot-tempered speech is many people's most common reaction to anger.

Many Old Testament proverbs comment on angry speech. It is "cruel" and "overwhelming" (Prov 27:4) and sits "in the lap of fools" (Eccl 7:9). "A quick-tempered man," says Proverbs 14:17, "does foolish things." Proverbs 29:22 says, "An angry man stirs up dissension, and a hot-tempered one commits many sins." Psalm 37:8 says, "Refrain from anger and turn from wrath; do not fret—it leads only to evil." Sirach 28:11 adds that "hasty quarreling kindles bloodshed."

A person who is angry is like a tornado or a volcano. We are never entirely sure how they will react, what they will do or say. "Hotheads" are dangerous to be near when they are about to explode. We find it unhelpful to talk to them or even stay near them until they calm down. In some cases, being with a person with a hot temper can be life-threatening. For this reason, a wise Jewish proverb provides this chilling warning:

Do not push a dispute with a quick-tempered man
    nor ride with him through the desert.
For bloodshed is nothing to him.

And when there is no one to help, he will destroy you.[24]
Ancient attempts to explain the person who flies off the handle rival those of modern psychology. Jewish rabbis suggest that such a person is either arrogant or forgetful.[25] Another rabbi suggests that the hot-tempered person feels tormented and miserable: "His life is not life."[26] Philo believes that the angry person's reason is unable to get a grip on his emotions.[27] Aristotle says that a quarrelsome person does not know how to make friends.[28]

We cannot help but get angry sometimes, and our anger needs to have an outlet. However, we can't use this as an excuse to let our lives become filled with unhealthy and unfair outbursts of anger. Flying off the handle becomes a habit, our way of dealing improperly with life's difficulties. This kind of lifestyle is contagious and can rub off on others, friends and family. Watch your friends' children—or your own. You will see that they cope with anger as their parents do, body posture and all. Dysfunctional ways of coping with anger are passed on from generation to generation. That's why they must be stopped. Proverbs 22:24-25 observes the bad modeling in hot-tempered individuals and wisely recommends:

Do not make friends with a hot-tempered man,
> do not associate with one easily angered,
or you may learn his ways
> and get yourself ensnared.

What if we are already friends with someone prone to excessive anger? What should we do? Seneca, a first-century Roman philosopher who wrote an entire book on anger, makes a time-worn suggestion that sounds like advice many of us received from our mothers. He recommends "challenging him with kindness" when the hot-tempered person goes on a rampage against you. "Animosity," he says, "if abandoned by one side, dies forthwith; it takes two to make a fight."[29]

Seneca's advice may seem trite and even be inappropriate (or dangerous) in some cases, such as that of a woman married to a verbally abusive man. Nevertheless, our experience tells us his counsel is often true. When others are blowing off anger on us, our angry response somehow seems to justify their anger to themselves. They have provoked us to behave as badly as they do. Our natural response to become angry also has a tendency to escalate the quarrel, like adding gasoline to a fire. A true friend will avoid getting drawn into an angry outburst and will wait until the angry person is ready to talk about his feelings calmly. We may even need to stay away from him for a while. Anger is a good attention-getter; it can call attention to a problem, but it is never a path to solution.

One day a few years ago, as I was leaving our house, my next-door neighbor's car roared into his driveway. I waved "hi" as I usually do, but I could see fire in his eyes. He was boiling over as he got out of the car, and I was flabbergasted to discover that his wrath was kindled at me. Fortunately, he never struck me, but he shouted over and over again that my son had struck his son and even though I was there at the time, I hadn't done anything about it. His wife had called him at work.

He certainly got my attention, but resolution came only when—as calmly as I could—I was able to convince him that he had received wrong information. His son had not been socked in the stomach but slapped on his bottom. In fact, his son's behavior in our yard had been totally out of control and inappropriate. Furthermore, I had already disciplined my son for his action.

The New Testament gives similar advice for dealing with people who are angry with us. Romans 12:17 directs Christians not to "repay anyone evil for evil." Verse 19 continues, "Do not take revenge, my friends, but leave room for God's wrath." Paul then quotes Proverbs 25:21-22, which concludes with "In doing this, you will heap burning coals on his head." The image of the coals does not mean further inflaming the person's anger, but searing his conscience and helping him come to his senses. When we respond in kindness to an angry outburst, we are helping our friend realize the foolishness of what he is saying. Paul finishes by admonishing, "Do not be overcome by evil, but overcome evil with good" (v. 21).

The New Testament also calls us to control our own anger. Two different words are primarily involved. Both are used to describe God's wrath in judgment of sinful humankind. Both are also used of human anger and the angry speech that often coincides with the emotion. One of the words, *thumos,* is related to the Latin word *fumus,* meaning "smoke" or "steam," from which English gets the word *fume* to describe the passionate emotion of anger. The slight distinction in this Greek word is its use to describe situations in which sudden outbursts of anger occur, as in Luke 4:28, where the people of Nazareth are characterized as "furious" just before they try to throw Jesus off a cliff. We sometimes visualize such situations by saying that someone "blew his top," or we even say that someone is "blowing off steam."

This word also occurs in 2 Corinthians 12:20, where Paul lists a number of disappointingly negative qualities he fears he may find in the Corinthian church when he makes a visit. This type of angry outburst has been displayed in a contemporary setting by the great tennis player John McEnroe, whose legendary tirades against match judges will forever taint his career.

The other word, *orgē,* tends to depict anger that is more brooding and results in more deliberate actions. It is used in 1 Timothy 2:8 in contrast to the positive action of prayer. Jesus uses the verb form of this word when he compares anger to murder. It involves cold, calculating vengeance.

These two words for anger occur side by side in both Colossians 3:8 and Ephesians 4:31. The NIV translates *thumos* "rage" and *orgē* "anger." Other translations use "wrath" or "passion" for *thumos* but stay with "anger" for *orgē.* The Ephesians passage includes a third word to refer to the shouting that is sometimes associated with anger. It is important to note that both kinds of anger are ruled out of bounds for Christians. Neither is acceptable behavior.

Pitting an author's choice of one of these words against other would lead us to misunderstand many New Testament passages. So when James 1:20 says, "Man's anger does not bring about the righteous life that God desires," using *orgē,* this does not imply that emotional outbursts of anger *(thumos)* are acceptable because they are somehow good catharsis. He means that any display of anger, whether it comes out of quick rage or out of a slow boil, falls outside the standard God has set for us by his own character. When James 1:19 says that a person should be "quick to listen, slow to speak and slow to become angry," it is not advocating angry display as long as it comes slowly. Rather, it offers proverbial wisdom to keep us from any angry display.

Despite the condemnation of anger in the New Testament, Ephesians

4:26 recognizes a distinction between the emotion of anger and the sinful actions that might result from our anger when it says, "In your anger do not sin." Feelings of anger in response to a hurt someone causes us are to be expected as we deal with the real world around us. God, after all, has created us with our emotions. However, what we do about our anger is what's critical. Anything we do or say that stems from uncontrolled, unexamined and unrepented anger is sin. It goes against the righteous character God patterns for us. So the modern concept of venting our anger on someone for our own emotional health is not condoned by Scripture. Rather, our anger should be a signal of a problem requiring our serious attention. Maybe we have a case against someone that we need to figure out how to deal with. Maybe our anger is covering our embarrassment over something stupid that we did, and we need to give ourselves some time out to discover this. Maybe we are just tired or sick and need to go to bed.

If we are going to vent our anger, we should do it in the form of prayer to God, who can help us pinpoint the problem and decide what course of action is needed. Maybe we need to do something physical, like running or walking, to drain off the emotional energy. In any case, when Ephesians 4:26 says, "Do not let the sun go down while you are still angry," it is telling us to do something constructive to rid ourselves of anger before we do something we will regret. Ephesians 4:27 explains that this is vital because otherwise we "give the devil a foothold." Uncontrolled anger will lead us into sin.

One is hard-pressed to find biblical warrant for rationalizing any of our angry displays as "righteous indignation." When the Bible talks about God's anger toward human beings, it refers to God's unique ability to judge and condemn us for our sin. It is not remotely comparable to out-of-control emotional displays of human beings, which always result in sinful words or actions. God may very well be passionate in his disappointment in us and in his hatred of our sin. However, the words and actions he takes come from a deep love for us. He warns us not to sin over and over and over. He also sent his Son as a unique sacrifice to die for our sin and make it possible for us to be totally forgiven and live forever with him.

We trivialize Jesus' action of clearing the outer temple courtyard of moneychangers (Mt 21:12-13; Mk 11:15-18; Lk 19:45-48; Jn 2:13-22) if we use this biblical incident to justify a tirade against our children for leaving their toys on the stairs or even screaming a right-to-life slogan at a pregnant woman entering an abortion clinic. Being right does not make a blind display of anger right. What Jesus did in clearing the courtyard of the Gentiles was a carefully calculated protest symbolizing God's judgment on the Jews for denying Gentiles the opportunity to come to God. It was not a fit of rage. Mark 11:11 makes this clear when it says that the day before, Jesus had come to the temple and had "looked around at everything." His anger was kindled then. The action came after a night of prayerful consideration of what to do.

Be Spiritually Alert

As we conclude this chapter, it is important to remind ourselves that simply labeling sins does not remove them from our behavior pattern. Still, knowing the biblical stance on tactlessness, gossip, mockery and hot-tempered speech can help alert our mind and our spirit to just how wrong these ways of talking are. Awareness of sin can and should initiate repentance and real steps to change. If we listen to the Spirit within us, we do have the power to use our speech more and more for God's glory than for hurting others around us.

Daily Speech Sins

Shades of Falsehood

S ome sins of speech are not accidental blunders but rather are intentionally false. With full knowledge of what we are doing, we give someone wrong information or the impression that matters are quite different from the way they really are. At bottom, this is lying. However, this chapter will also address certain distinctive kinds of lying like slander, deceit, flattery and boasting.

Lying

"Lying is a just a way of life," announces a 1992 article in *USA Today*. The article summarizes the key survey findings of a book entitled *The Day America Told the Truth*. One of the authors, James Patterson, is quoted as saying, "Americans are willing to lie at the drop of a hat. Lying is part of their lives." The survey reports that 91 percent of people living in the United States acknowledge that they lie routinely. Eighty-six percent lie regularly to parents, 75 percent to friends, 73 percent to brothers and sisters, 69 percent to spouses. That amounts to a lot of lying going on every day in our homes and workplaces.

Although the news is shocking, it shouldn't surprise us that much. In fact, the Bible would suggest that those 9 percent who say they don't lie are lying. Psalm 116:11 says, "All men are liars," and Psalm 12:2 says, "Everyone lies to his neighbor." The Bible does its part to demonstrate the truth of this assessment of humankind, too, by portraying frankly the lies and deceptions of its characters.

Genesis tells of the serpent's lie to Eve—that God had lied to her about the tree of the knowledge of good and evil (3:4), of Adam's, and then Cain's, attempts to deceive God (3:10; 4:9). It also tells of Abraham and Isaac's attempt to deceive others into thinking their wives were their sisters (12:13; 20:2; 26:7). Jacob deceives Isaac, with encouragement from his mother (27:19). Rachel lies to her father, Laban, about taking the household idols with her (31:35). Jacob's sons lie to him about Joseph's death (37:29-35). Under David's influence, Jonathan deceives his father, Saul. David lies to Ahimelech, the priest of Nob, thereby contributing to his death. David deceives Achish, the king of Gath, by feigning madness, and then later lies about his raiding expeditions (1 Sam 20:1-10; 21:1-6; 22:11-19; 21:10-15; 27:1-12).

The prophets depict Israel as a nation of liars and abounding in people who love falsehood. Isaiah 59:3-4 lambastes them:

Your lips have spoken lies,
   and your tongue mutters wicked things.
No one calls for justice;
   no one pleads his case with integrity.
They rely on empty arguments and speak lies;
   they conceive trouble and give birth to evil.

Jeremiah (5:1-3, 30-31) seeks vainly for someone who speaks truth and comes to the terrifying conclusion that even the prophets and priests of God speak falsely—and the people love it. (See also Jer 9:1-9; Hos 11:12; 12:1.)

The analysis of the wizened Jewish rabbi is right: "Falsehood is frequent, truth is rare."[1] It is true in the Old Testament. It is true today. It will always be true.

Jimmy Carter, who became president based on the campaign pledge "I will never lie to the American people," found out just how difficult that promise was to keep in the swirl of events in the Oval Office. No doubt he was confronted hourly with information and issues that challenged that promise.

None of us may face the particular challenge of being head of state, but challenges to avoid lying or to avoid being less than truthful flood our lives. Will I lie to cover for my boss or coworker? Do I tell my spouse what I really paid for that expensive item I couldn't resist? How can I tell my parents the truth about some of my extracurricular activities while I am away at college? How much do I tell my children?

One young Christian woman faced the challenge of lying and deception in the business practices of her employer. In a new job as the marketing representative for an industrial medical clinic, Jane soon found that her job required her to bill companies for more expensive claims than the services performed and to flat-out lie about company practices in order to sign new clients. Refusing to do this, she was fired.[2]

We must be prepared, as Jane was, to pay the consequences of telling the truth in a society whose engine seems to run on deception. Oliver North lied to Congress because he believed it was in the best interests of the country. Ivan Boesky bilked hundreds of customers of their money. Over a thousand public officials were prosecuted and convicted in 1990.[3] And then there are you and I, who also lie but are not in the public eye and are not usually caught.

Most of us learned the benefits of lying as children. This is not an excuse, but it does show how ingrained the practice is in us. One study shows that most children are lying by the time they are two, and by age six all are lying.[4] We learn that people will think better of us if they don't know the truth, and we learn that we can avoid punishment.

The analysis of the early Jewish writer Philo is telling. He suggests that at best our speech is only partly true and partly false.[5] He views the root of the problem in the fact that speech requires a blending of our rational and physical capacities, the latter of which he considers totally corrupt. Christian writer Francis Schaeffer contends, however, that the problem is much deeper than our corrupted bodies.[6] The problem lies in our inner selves, but not just at our conscious level. It goes beyond where we can mentally reach, to our subconscious. Nothing we say or do occurs with pure motives. Despite our best conscious intentions, unconsciously we are always looking out for number one, whether that means receiving greater rewards or avoiding punishment.

We may not be able to do much about our unconscious motives. We can trust that the Holy Spirit is working with us at that level. But ample room remains for us to improve on the conscious level, to overcome our attraction to lying. Hearing what the Bible says about lying should help.

The first thing we must realize is just how wrong lying is. According to Proverbs 12:22, "The LORD detests lying lips." In Proverbs 6:16-19, seven items appear on a list of things that the Lord hates; two of these are "a lying tongue" and "a false witness who pours out lies." The lying of human beings stands over against God's own character, according to Numbers 23:9.

Second, the fleeting nature of the benefits of lying must penetrate our thick skulls. Many lies are discovered and punished. North and Boesky went to prison. And even those lies that are not discovered by society will be known by God, and we will be punished for them. Psalm 5:6 says of God, "You destroy those who tell lies." That goes not just for individuals but also for nations. Micah 6:13 states bluntly that it was for the sins of false speech that Israel was being destroyed.

Third, Satan is the prince of liars, and when we lie we help establish his dark kingdom and erode the kingdom of God (Jn 8:38; 13:2; Acts 5:3; 13:10; Rev 12:9). Judas, Ananias and Elymas are a few of those notorious in the New Testament for opening themselves up to the influence of Satan and telling lies in order to subvert God's efforts to redeem the world. When you and I lie, it may seem minor sometimes, but in reality we are scoring a goal for Satan's team. In doing so, we are hurting the efforts of our own team and betraying God. As Ephesians 6:12 emphasizes, "Our struggle is . . . against the powers of this dark world." A crucial part of that struggle is in the moral arena of lying.

Fourth, truthful speech is supposed to be a critical sign of the change from our old way of life to our new life in Christ. Colossians 3:9-10 stresses this point: "Do not lie to each other, since you have taken off your old self with its practices and have put on the new self, which is being renewed in knowledge in the image of its Creator."

Truthful speech is also vital to the unity that binds together the Christian community. Ephesians 4:25 says, "Each of you must put off falsehood and speak truthfully to his neighbor, for we are all members of one body."

Slander

Like gossip, slander involves repeating information behind a person's back. In gossip the chief fault is the repetition of confidential information without taking responsibility for whether the information is true or false. In slander someone purposely spreads distorted information about someone else in order to discredit them. Motivated by jealousy, quest for power, money, job advancement or just plain dislike for someone, the slanderer desires to sway public opinion against a person. As Ezekiel 22:9 describes them, slanderers are "bent on shedding blood." Slander is lying with the unmitigated intention of hurting someone.

In order to avoid printing slander, legitimate newspapers abide by a policy of not printing articles about people that are not backed by at least two sources. If they do print an article that wrongly defames the character of someone, they can be sued for libel. This is rare. However, supermarket tabloids are often sued for libel, because they will happily print an unsupported rumor that will titillate their readers. They make so much money in sales that the lawsuits, although an irritant, do not stop them. Slander sells.

These two spectrums in printed news symbolize the field of personal relationships too. Some people care about others enough to take it upon themselves to squelch nasty false rumors. Other people feed on slander and multiply its harm. As Christians, we must take our place among those who care about others enough to defend their honor in the face of those who would devour them. As the Jewish Talmud says, "Whoever relates slander and whoever accepts slander . . . against his neighbor, deserves to be cast to the dogs."[7]

The ninth commandment in Exodus 20:16, "You shall not give false testimony against your neighbor," unequivocally condemns slander both in the courtroom and in personal relationships. Jewish thinkers describe slander as "more vicious—than the transgressions which are called 'great': idolatry, adultery, and murder."[8] We might wonder what kind of reasoning could hold a verbal sin like slander to be worse than physically taking someone's life. The rabbis' reasoning, explained in numerous places,[9] is that slander is capable of killing three people in one thrust: the slanderer and the person who listens to and accepts the slander receive God's judgment; the innocent victim may be sentenced to death for a crime, or his or her reputation may be irreparably damaged in the public eye.

The reasoning of the Greek orator Isocrates is similar:

I do not wonder that men complain that slander is the greatest evil. What, indeed, could work more mischief? It causes liars to be looked on with respect, innocent men to be regarded as criminals, and judges to violate their oaths. In a word, it smothers truth, and in pouring false ideas into our ears, it leaves no man among our citizens secure from unjust death.[10]

People are vulnerable to slander. Was Clarence Thomas guilty of sexually harassing Anita Hill, or was this slander? Whatever the truth, the allegations sullied the character not only of Thomas and Hill but also of those politicians who bumbled their way through the 1991 hearings.

God takes slander seriously. Jeremiah and Ezekiel, in fact, cite rampant slander as one of the reasons for Israel's destruction and exile (Jer 6:28; 9:4; Ezek 22:4). Proverbs 21:28 says that "a false witness will perish," and Psalms 101:5 says that God will put the slanderer "to silence."

The rabbis further capture the seriousness with which God views slander when they describe how God afflicts slanderers with croup and leprosy and the lands they live in with plagues, drought and the departure of God's presence.[11] Slanderers will be cast into Gehinnon.[12] Just as God cut out the serpent's tongue, so will he do to those of us who commit slander.[13]

In the New Testament, slander appears on most of the sin lists. It has the dubious honor of being the most commonly named speech sin in the New Testament, occurring at least eighteen times. For Christians, the New Testament alarm is loud and clear: we are not to participate in such harmful talk, which, in fact, characterizes the ungodly.

A number of different words are employed to convey the idea of slander.[14] One of the words literally means "speak against" but is usually translated more specifically as "slander." Paul uses this word along with many others in Romans 1:30 to exemplify the depravity of humankind without God. In 2 Corinthians 12:20, Paul uses this word again, among others, to portray the kind of ungodly behavior he fears he may find if he returns to Corinth personally. First Peter 2:1 implores us to leave behind the kind of immature speech behavior this word conveys so we can move on to Christian maturity.

Another word for slander is used in Colossians 3:9 in a list of many old, earthly ways of life that Paul begs his readers to abandon. This word is usually translated "blasphemy" when the context indicates that defamation of God's character is in mind.

A third word used for slander is found in 2 Timothy 3:3, among other words listed for the purpose of depicting the evil of people in the last days. This word also comes up thirty-five times as one of the names for Satan in the New Testament.

Although the word for slander does not appear in Matthew 7:1-2, it is probably the most prominent of all the speech sins that this commonly quoted saying of Jesus implicitly condemns. "Do not judge, or you too will be judged!" demands that Jesus' disciples withhold criticism of others. Unbridled criticism can quickly lead to slander.

The implicit connection between this teaching of Jesus and slander is made explicit in James 4:11-12. After pleading for Christians not to "slander one another," James lays out his reasoning. First, he says that when we slander a Christian brother, we slander God's law and judge it. James reaches behind the spoken act of slander to the judgmental thoughts that precipitate it. He informs us that judgmental thoughts not only strike out at a fellow Christian but also strike out at the law. We do injury to the law as we sidestep it or kick it in the corner in order to harm someone with our speech.

James's second point, then, is that such action puts us above the law rather than under it as we are supposed to be. We are "sitting in judgment on it" when we are supposed to be "keeping it," as James says.

Third, James says that in doing this we have put ourselves in a harrowing predicament. We have dared sit down in a place reserved for only one person, *the* Lawgiver and Judge. The only one qualified to judge the law is the One in whom it originates. Only God administers it for deliverance or destruction.

So James's fourth point, in the form of a rhetorical question, "Who are you to judge your neighbor?" is intended to blast us out of God's chair to our proper position—on our knees before the Almighty. The bottom line is that when we slander our brother or sister, we slander—even blaspheme—God by behaving as gods over the law.

The question about what law James has in mind here is not clarified until the last word of verse 12, "neighbor." This distinctive word choice connects us to the law of neighbor love, "Love your neighbor as yourself." The command is found in various forms all over the New Testament.[15] Quite understandably, James intertwines the notion of judging one another with loving our neighbor, because he believes Jesus viewed the two as complementary sides of the same principle on which believers are to order their lives. Loving our neighbors—and our fellow Christians—means that we are not to judge them or speak against them. We must not participate in spreading false rumors about them.

We have probably all have been victims of slander. Our first wave of anger, once we find out about it, is directed at the person who began spreading the false stories about us. However, when we are honest with ourselves, we know we all have enemies, and such people can be expected to try to get at us. Our second wave of anger comes out of a deeper hurt and focuses on all those people—our friends, neighbors, relatives and colleagues—who accepted the false rumor about us at face value. We wonder how they could possibly think that we would say or do such a thing. We wonder why they didn't try to quell the rumor, confront the slanderer or talk to us sooner. Slander is so deadly that relationships can be shattered even when the slanderer is exposed.

For us Christians, our job not only is to avoid initiating slander but also to guard against spreading slander. We need to give people the benefit of the doubt. We need to defend the person slandered, bring the rumor to them and let them respond. We need to expose the slanderer, confront them with their sin and try to bring about reconciliation. Slander is deadly, and we must not hesitate to act as loving police to protect and defend one another from it.

Deceit

Lying, slander and deceit have the same objective: to make someone believe something to be true that, in fact, is not. Lying and slander involve making false statements. Deceit employs a broad array of tactics that include lying but also speech that could be described as misleading or coy. Deceit could even employ silence, conveniently allowing people to believe what they want to believe rather than stating the truth.

If a police officer is chasing my friend down the street, I can choose to help my friend by deceiving the officer in a number of ways. I can step forward and direct the officer the wrong way. I can flat-out lie if the officer asks me if he went "thataway." I can pretend that I didn't see my friend pass and hope the officer chooses the wrong direction. I can even distract the officer from the pursuit by faking a heart attack or making up an incident that the officer will have to investigate rather than chase my friend.

Probably, our most prevalent exposure to deceit is in advertising and sales. We are bombarded with television commercials that try to make us think that a certain product is the best or that our life will be so much better if we have the product. A series of 1992 commercials by Anheuser Busch tried to convince us that popping open a Bud Light made one a real mountain man, of course with the customary string of attractive women hanging on him. The late-night car dealer comes on to convince us that he has the lowest prices ever—weekend after weekend after weekend—when at best he may have one or two cars at the prices that fill our television screen. The persistent salesperson comes to our door or—more likely these days—solicits us over the phone, telling us we have just won something. I chuckle at the home-improvement callers who begin by saying, "We are currently working in your area." If they really were, they wouldn't be calling; they would know that vinyl siding and thermal windows are standard on all the homes in our subdivision.

When Gavin, one of my sons, was only eight, he learned to distrust commercials because of the deception in them. While cleaning the base-ment, he came upon the broken pieces of a super airplane glider he had paid sixteen dollars to purchase a year earlier. Looking at them, he said, "Oh, yeah, I remember. They made it look like it could do neat things on the commercial, but when I tried to do them, it hit the ground and broke."

A more subtle form of deceitful advertising involves product labeling. As of May 22, 1992, the Food and Drug Administration ordered Procter & Gamble to remove the word *fresh* from its Citrus Hill Fresh Choice orange juice because it was made from concentrate and water like every other orange-juice product on the shelf.

Such tactics in merchandising are ageless. One traveler to Greece in the sixth century B.C. noted the stark inconsistency between Greek philosophy and Greek commerce by asking, "How is it that the Greeks prohibit falsehood and yet obviously tell falsehoods in retail trade?"[16] And so it continues, and we must be ever aware when we shop.

Probably the most common form of deceit you and I participate in is cheating. As children, we learned to cheat at games by peeking at the cards, moving the checker or changing the rules to our advantage. Our playmate's home run is disallowed because we had forgotten to mention that the tree it hit is out of play. Tagging someone's coat is the same as tagging them, even if they couldn't feel it. Our success at cheating encourages us to use it in the classroom when we can't remember how to spell a word on the spelling test, but we can see it on our neighbor's paper. In adulthood, the impulse to cheat comes readily in our income taxes, our lunch breaks at work and our marital relationship.

Cheating is epidemic in our society. An article in *USA Today* headlines: "Cheating Is Basic Course in College."[17] Reporting the results of a survey conducted by Donald McCabe, associate professor of business ethics at Rutgers University, of six thousand students at elite universities, it found that 67 percent admitted to cheating. Breaking the survey down by majors, it showed that business majors were the worst, at 87 percent, while humanities majors were the best, at 63 percent.

What's wrong with cheating and deception? For one thing, Psalm 12:1-3 ranks it with lying and condemns it. For another thing, as one Jewish rabbi says, it is thievery.[18] By deceit, a person is gaining something that doesn't belong to them, whether it be money, a good grade, success or respect.

Also, in many instances the deceiver ends up hurting others. An excellent example of this is found in the apocryphal addition to Daniel, unfortunately not known to Protestants very well, called "The Virtue of Susannah." It tells of two seditious elders of the people who lusted after the beautiful and virtuous wife of Joachim. One day, when they caught Susannah alone in the garden bathing, they propositioned her. Because she refused them, and to keep her from publicly exposing them, they charged her with adultery, knowing that their testimony would be honored over hers.

Having been found guilty by the council, Susannah prayed earnestly to God for help. He sent Daniel, who reopened the trial. Daniel questioned the old men separately and asked each of them exactly where in the garden they had seen Susannah's adultery take place. Unable to consult with each other, they named different locations and thus revealed themselves to be perjurers. By Jewish law, they received the same sentence of execution they had tried deceptively to bring down on Susannah.

We don't usually think about hurting others when we deceive. Usually we are concentrating on what we will gain. Yet cheating on income taxes takes away money that might have gone to a program for the poor in Mississippi. On a curve, our undeserved high grade may cut someone else out of a grade they deserve. The promotion we win by guile leaves someone else in the dust.

The New Testament treats deceit as a type of speech that has the ability to pull off the ultimate heist and bring about the worst possible hurt. It condemns deceptive teaching that can lure believers away to eternal death. Romans 16:17-18 speaks of those who by their "smooth talk and flattery . . . deceive the minds of naive people." Ephesians 5:6 warns us, "Let no one deceive you with empty words, for because of such things God's wrath comes on those who are disobedient." The deceitful teaching about which the New Testament warns is not just a matter of doctrine. It is also concerns threats against the moral standards promoted by Christianity.[19] Galatians 6:7-10 particularly cautions us not to be deceived into thinking that our behavior does not matter. Rather, we must "please the

Spirit" and not "become weary in doing good."

Daily, the world confronts you and me with deceit: consumer deceit, relational deceit, lifestyle deceit, religious deceit. People, products and ideas endeavor to distract us from what is true and corral us into their deceit. If we intend to set foot outside our house or turn on the television, we had better beware. And we need to confront our own desire to make people think we are something we are not. That's the truly hidden harm of deceit. We might come to believe our own press. That will inevitably lead to a hard fall when we bump up against reality.

Flattery

Flattery is a particular form of deceit. In flattering us, people stroke our ego for ulterior motives. Our hunger to be liked and respected makes us all vulnerable to the sugarcoated compliments that flatterers dish out. We fail to see that flatterers don't mean what they say—I suppose that sometimes we don't even care. Flatterers want something from us that they don't deserve—maybe our trust, maybe our money, maybe our influence. But flatterers' inability to approach us honestly makes anything they might gain from us hollow. When we discover we have been taken in by a flatterer, we are crushed, humiliated, because our privacy has been invaded. We have welcomed someone into our lives whose real intention was to use us.

Flatterers flock to people with high visibility: celebrities, politicians, athletes. Yes-men and groupies who will do anything to get a video part engulf rock stars like Michael Jackson and Madonna. Campaign workers coo for a candidate because they hope that victory will mean a political appointment. People who seem to require ego pumping in order to have the confidence to do what they already do well make themselves incredibly vulnerable to flatterers on the make.

Any of us with low self-esteem is susceptible to the wiles of the flatterer. A wealthy but insecure widow is "easy pickin's" for a cunning suitor. An unhappy fourteen-year-old girl is ill-equipped to fend off the compliments of a young man with only one thing on his mind. An overweight, balding executive in the throes of midlife crisis may be all too responsive to the charms of his attractive young secretary.

We must guard against falling prey to flattery, because in the end it will hurt us immensely. Proverbs 26:28 says that "a flattering mouth works ruin," and Proverbs 29:5 declares that "whoever flatters his neighbor is spreading a net for his feet." In the Apocrypha, Sirach 12:16-17 adds that the sweet-speaking flatterer will "knock you into a pit." The point is that eventually the true motives of the flatterer will reveal themselves. She may finally get all she wants out of us or become frustrated. Then she will turn on us and tell us what she really thinks of us. She will hurt us all she can.

In *The Lion, the Witch and the Wardrobe* by C. S. Lewis, the Queen of Narnia, a witch, makes Edmund think she likes him by giving him Turkish delight—a sugary treat—and promising that he will be Prince of Narnia, but only if he delivers his older brother and sisters to her. When he shows up at her castle without them, saying they are close by, she is cross with him and realizes that she has gotten all the use out of him that she can. On the way to hunt down his siblings, she strikes him with a vicious blow when he complains about her turning a squirrel family into stone. When the snow melts so that the witch's sleigh cannot go, she binds Edmund as a slave as they continue walking. When they stop, his ropes are removed, and he hears the sound of a knife being sharpened. Edmund is to be killed by the witch for treachery, and she is only prevented by Aslan, the lion Christ-figure, who offers himself in exchange.

The Jewish rabbis observe that flatterers cut away at the moral fabric of a society. Eventually the hole can become so large that the society becomes vulnerable to the attacks of its enemies.[20] Specifically, it is noted that the Israelites' flattery of Herod Agrippa contributed to their destruction by Rome.[21] When too many people are looking out for number one and seeking only to get all they can for themselves, the culture at large will go to pot. Such a commentary on first-century Israel very well may fit the tombstone of twentieth-century Western culture.

The first-century Greek moralist Plutarch calls flatterers "bastard members of the human race."[22] He does so because a flatterer perverts the most basic level of trust that bonds humanity together. Communication becomes a circus if flattery prevails. Plutarch devotes an entire essay in his writings to helping us separate flattery from frankness, friendship from verbal prostitution.[23] His opening remarks in this essay, describing the moral harm flattery does to an individual, match up to anything in contemporary psychology: "The flatterer always takes a position over against the maxim 'Know thyself' by creating in every man deception towards himself and ignorance both of himself and of the good and evil that concerns himself; the good he renders defective and incomplete, and the evil wholly impossible to amend."[24]

Flattery believed makes us vain and conceited. We become impenetrable to the truth about ourselves. It also detracts us from developing our real strengths. They are left standing like the half-completed buildings in a construction site that ran out of investors.

A young man believes his coach, his dad and his friends, who keep telling him he can make it in major-league baseball. He abandons college, where he was excelling in math, and for eight years toils in the minor leagues, never getting out of double-A ball. By then he is married, with children, and the opportunity for college is gone.

The story could be told the other way around. It doesn't matter. Over and over people like you and me are cozened by others into ambitions that should not be ours. In doing so, we squander what God actually has given us. In Jesus' parable of the talents, the owner took away the talent from the servant who did not invest it (Mt 25:14-30).

Plutarch displays his outrage over a situation that plagued his society as it does ours. He inveighs against "parasites" who prey on young people and turn them against their parents.[25] The American record industry makes millions inciting the anger of young people against parents and adult society in general. Videos capitalize on the natural wedge between independence-seeking teens and their concerned parents by portraying parents as out-of-touch fools. A 1992 rap song by Ice T called "Cop Killer," written after the Los Angeles riots, encouraged black youth to kill police. These music products not only tap the anger of youth but also flatter youth into thinking they are wiser, stronger and more correct than they really are. These artists pretend to be the friends of youth but really just want their money and their adulation. Philo is right when he calls flattery "diseased friendship."[26] It brings out the worst rather than developing the best in people as true friendship should.

God despises flattery because it is so harmful to us and hampers us in reaching our potential for him. Samson ruined not only his life but also the lives of the Israelites he was sworn to protect when he succumbed to Delilah's flattery. Imagine how the fortunes of the Hebrews would have been lost had Joseph given in to the spicy words of Potiphar's wife. Thus in Psalm 12:3-5 God agrees to "cut off all flattering lips." His judgment will fall heavily on flatterers.

In Mark 10:17, Jesus provides us a poignant example of how to deal with flattery. The rich young ruler approaches him with a seemingly harmless question, "What shall I do to inherit eternal life?" But hidden in the question is a desire to secure Jesus' blessing on his life as it is, because he thinks he has already done plenty to gain eternal life. Probably he had always been told he was a good little boy, and he grew into a handsome, clean-cut man who diligently kept the commandments as he knew them, better than anyone else around.

He tries to get the blessing he thinks he deserves by flattering Jesus, addressing him as "good teacher" (v. 17). To Jesus, this gives the young man's game away, and he calls him on it. First, he tries to point him to the source and epitome of all "goodness." "No one is good—except God alone," Jesus says. Measured against God, none of us is good. Jesus then exposes the limitations of the young man's goodness when he challenges him to sell everything he has and give it to the poor (v. 21). Will he sacrifice all that he has for the benefit of others as God does and is in fact doing at that moment in the person of Jesus before him? No. His very source of "goodness" is his wealth, which gives him an easy life with few moral and spiritual challenges—not God.

The overconfident young man walks away sad. Maybe he now has a more realistic view of himself. Perhaps he eventually even learns the same lesson that you and I must learn about dealing with the false floor that flattery puts under our feet. Chuck Colson argues that the greatest myth of the twentieth century is that people think they are good.[27] But all flattery—including self-flattery—fails if we keep gauging our life against the righteousness of God rather than that of human beings. This is why Jesus could so easily deflect the young man's attempts to flatter him. He knew where he stood in relationship to God.

Second, any achievement in our life comes through God. When an athlete like 1992 Olympic one-hundred-meter gold medalist Gail Devers consciously remembers to give praise to God for her victory when the microphone is thrust into her face, she protects herself from believing the false flattery of the reporters. That is why she could so easily shrug off what appeared to reporters as a devastating, stumbling fifth-place finish of the two-hundred-meter hurdles that she led until her front foot crashed into a gate and sent her sprawling. Humility in success will keep us from humiliation in failure.

After all this, we may begin to wonder whether we should even compliment people at all. One Jewish rabbi, in fact, says we should not. Others are so concerned about the evils of flattery that they seriously discuss whether a bride who is lame or blind should be told she is pretty.[28] Plato, who ardently defends the importance of honesty, admits, however, that physicians and politicians must sometimes paint unrealistically rosy pictures for the overall good of their patients and subjects.[29]

All encouragement and praise are not flattery. Flattery's intention is harmful and fraudulent. We need to be positive and to encourage one another, but honesty draws boundaries regarding just how glowing we can be. We want to help people achieve what God has in mind for them without leading them to become egotistical, overconfident and unrealistic.

You and I need to watch out for flatterers, wherever they may be—at home, at the job or at church. Let's accept compliments politely but also take the opportunities to point our admirers, whether sincere or insincere, to our heavenly Father.

Boasting

Boasting could be described as self-flattery. We tell others just how wonderful we are, usually without concern to avoid exaggeration. We want to impress others so badly that we enlarge our good characteristics and accomplishments and shrink our failings. We present what we wish were true about ourselves. We make the most out of actual achievements.

One of the ways we are most tempted to brag involves our associations. We like to make hay out of having known or at least met famous people. Perhaps someone says they really enjoyed Kevin Costner in *Dances with Wolves,* and we smugly say, "Oh, Kevin's a really nice guy. I met him once," or "He's the nephew of a friend of my mother's cousin." Someone might mention a great baseball player like Bobby Bonilla or Roger Clemens, and we promptly pipe in that our uncle coached him back when he was a Little Leaguer, our boss at work went to the same high school as he did, or we have his rookie baseball card. We think this will lead others to see us as bigger or better, as if the greatness of these people somehow rubbed off on us because of these insignificant contacts.

We boast about "our team," whether it be the White Sox or the Mets; we boast that our team has the best defense or the best manager, or that its stadium has the best hot dogs. High-schoolers fight with their cross-town rivals because both boast that their school is the best in town. Parents boast about their children's accomplishments. "She's already potty-trained." "He's in the gifted class." "She's a cheerleader." "He's shortstop on the baseball team."

Probably the most famous boaster is heavyweight champion boxer Muhammad Ali, who dared to say, "I am the greatest." However, John Lennon came pretty close when he said that the Beatles were more popular than Jesus Christ.

In the Bible, the boaster who most readily comes to mind is Goliath in 1 Samuel 17. Actually, the most infamous boaster in the Bible is Sennacherib, the king of Assyria, who not only boasts of his nation's prowess against the Israelites but thumbs his nose at God as well.[30] Through his messenger to Hezekiah, he disdainfully assaults God and his power to rescue his people. He even insists that God himself has ordained the capture of Jerusalem by his hands. Through Isaiah in 2 Kings 19:20-34, God reviews the boasting insults of Sennacherib: that with the might of his chariots he has "ascended . . . the utmost heights of Lebanon, . . . cut down its tallest cedars . . . dug wells in foreign lands and . . . dried up all the streams of Egypt." Actually, God tells Sennacherib, all these things were possible only because of God's help. Because of Sennacherib's insolence, God now says,

"I will put my hook in your nose and my bit in your mouth, and I will make you return by the way you came."

In Isaiah 10:15, still speaking of Sennacherib, God queries, "Does the . . . saw boast against him who uses it?" God vows, "Under his pomp a fire will be kindled. . . . And the remaining trees of his forests will be so few that a child could write them down" (vv. 16, 19).

We can certainly learn from the example of Sennacherib that God does not like boasting and will punish it. Sennacherib also shows us, however, that the Bible associates boasting with the sin of blasphemy and views blasphemy as rooted in pride. In 2 Kings 19:22, Isaiah asks:

Who is it you have insulted and blasphemed?

Against whom have you raised your voice

and lifted your eyes in pride?

Against the Holy One of Israel!

Admittedly, when we boast, most of us do not raise our fists to heaven and tell God we are greater than he is. Rather, we may make more subtle boasts to others around us. Part of our sin lies in our intention to make our listeners envious—a sin for them. Our boasting may also incite them to boast about themselves in defense. However, the deeper offense really is against God, because boasting is a verbal eruption of pride.

Pride is thinking better of ourselves than is justified. But it also involves believing that our accomplishments stem from our own efforts alone. When we believe this as we make our boasts, we are snubbing God, who makes all things possible. That is blasphemy. We have put ourselves in God's place. In effect, our boasting is praise and worship of ourselves as God rather than of the true God who alone deserves such praise.

Sirach 10:12 wisely observes that "the beginning of man's pride is to separate from God; from his Maker he withdraws his heart." The arrogant person, says an observant rabbi, has "thrown off the yoke of Heaven,"[31] for he dares to speak in the name of God. In boasting, we presume wrongly that God's special favor rests on us.[32]

According to the New Testament, boasting, and the attitude of arrogance that fosters it, is precisely the opposite of the humility that God wants us to cultivate. From Jesus comes the key principle that we are to learn, and upon which so many New Testament passages build: "Everyone who exalts himself will be humbled, but he who humbles himself will be exalted."[33] Jesus paints the enduring picture of this principle in the story of the Pharisee and the tax collector (Lk 18:9-14). Only the tax collector, who pleaded for mercy, "went home justified before God"—not the Pharisee, who boasted of his achievements to God.

Many New Testament passages focus on the Pharisees and the rich as most prone to boasting.[34] First John 2:16 associates boasting with worldliness, and 1 Corinthians 3:1-4 links it to quarreling and divisiveness in the Christian community (see also Rom 12:16; 1 Cor 13:4; Phil 2:2-3; Rev 18:11, 15, 19). Paul tends to connect boasting to the basic spiritual problem of people's rejection of God. For Christians, who know they are saved only by God's grace, any kind of boasting should be out of the question.[35] We know we are nothing apart from God.

James 4:13-17 stings us with this point when it says that our tendency to make plans for the future before seeking God's guidance is a form of boasting. James asks, "What is your life? You are a mist that appears for a little while and then vanishes." By putting us in our place against the backdrop of the universe—we are nothing more than a morning mist that is burned away by ten o'clock—James hopes to burst our self-inflated egos down to where they belong. "All such boasting," he concludes, "is evil."

The need to boast is at the heart of the human problem. We seek desperately to be admired by others, to be better than others. We project this need in boasting at every opportunity to help fill the void of distinctive, individual purpose that God has put in each of us. Pride and boasting may ease the pain of that void. However, God has intended that our search for purpose be satisfied only when we find him. When he fills that void, boasting and pride lose their purpose. We know who we are in God and know that we have value to him now and in eternity. His sacrifice of Jesus for us makes this perfectly clear. Our boasting and insecurity are replaced by the kind of humility and confidence we see Jesus display in the Gospels.

Philo says that God's purpose for requiring circumcision of the Jews was to banish pride.[36] For Christians, the cross serves this purpose. How can we possibly look at the cross and feel any self-pride? The cross tells us we are secure in Christ, but it also fosters a pervasive humility because we know our security is possible only because Jesus paid the price for us. That's why Paul says any boasting we do should be about what Christ has done. In Galatians 6:14, he says, "May I never boast except in the cross of our Lord Jesus Christ, through which the world has been crucified to me, and I to the world" (see also Rom 5:11; 1 Cor 13—14; 1 Cor 1:31 [Jer 9:23]).

Boasting about Christ is evangelism. Rather than boasting about other things, we should be telling our coworkers and neighbors who Jesus is and what he has done for them. As Christians, we are also in the perfect position to use the power of our words to boost the confidence of fellow Christians who suffer from low self-esteem at times despite their security in Christ. Philippians 2:3-4 calls us to model ourselves after Christ: "Do nothing out of selfish ambition or vain conceit, but in humility consider others better than yourselves. Each of you should look . . . to the interests of others."

Aristotle is right when he observes that boasting is lying.[37] We deceive others about ourselves when we boast. It is the worst form of lying, I suppose, because in a sense we are lying to ourselves too. As Christians, we simply have no need to do that to ourselves as others do. Displaying the kind of confidence in the identity that God gives us is a critical advertisement of Christianity to the world around us. They can see for themselves the day-to-day difference that Christian faith makes in us. Control of our boasting, then, will bring people to Christ.

Falsehood as Rebellion Against God

In a biblical sense we are all liars in our basic rebellion against God. To deny God his rightful place in our lives is to live a lie. God is real. He is our Creator. He expects our worship and obedience. However, this basic ingredient of rebellion in our sinful nature does come to the surface in a number of ways. Lying is the trademark of them all. Every time we lie, we display our open rebellion against God.

My son, when confronted, often will say, "I lied on accident." This is not possible. Lying is intentional. It is a choice to follow Satan and to snub God. Our only real hope for reform lies in following Jesus Christ, who calls us to the truth of his reforming gospel.

4

The Key to
the Ethics of Talk

Control

*M*any of us indulge ourselves at every opportunity. We gorge ourselves with food, drink, clothes, television, sports and sometimes even religion. Moderation does not come easily to us. Yet the foundational ethic of talk is self-control. Whoever we are, wherever we are, whatever we do, we must control our talk.

Disciplining our talk may be the ideal place to begin disciplining ourselves in other areas. I have heard of desperately obese people having their mouths wired shut to allow them to lose weight. I suppose we could do this to improve our speech ethics too. But such an approach to control would deal only with mechanics. It does not deal with the lack of discipline in our character. So this chapter will focus on the need for control in our speech and show us where to begin, acknowledging just how hard it is for us to control what we say.

The Need for Control

"He who guards his lips guards his life, but he who speaks rashly will come to ruin," Proverbs 13:3 warns. Controlling our speech is a key to preventing failure in life. And "come to ruin" implies that even if harmful speech helps us get ahead now, we won't get past the judgment of God. Jesus paints the picture even more starkly in Matthew 12:36-37: "But I tell you that men will have to give account on the day of judgment for every careless word they have spoken. For by your words you will be acquitted, and by your words you will be condemned."

Jesus speaks of uncontrolled words as "careless," a word often used in Greek to describe someone who is lazy and unemployed. Just as a person without purpose and direction makes mischief and trouble, so do our mouths if they are not supervised. We are responsible for *every* word, Jesus emphasizes. One day God will judge and condemn us for those destructive words we have left unguarded and allowed to escape to do injury.

Jesus depicts us in a courtroom, compelled to muster a defense before a judge for each errant word. Can we "acquit" ourselves with more words? Perhaps you weren't feeling well when you screamed at your son. Perhaps I misunderstood my colleague's actions when I spread rumors about her. Realistically, though, you and I cannot justify all our errant words, and we are better off using our words before God to admit our guilt and plead for forgiveness. Our words are a window into our hearts, Jesus observes in the preceding verses, Matthew 12:33-35. So they are proper indicators for assessing our sinful character.

Other New Testament passages recognize that control of speech is at the forefront of our battle against sin as well as heading God's assessment of our sin. First Peter 3:10 admonishes, quoting Psalm 34:12-13,

> Whoever would love life
>> and see good days
> must keep his tongue from evil
>> and his lips from deceitful speech.

Within a three-part proverb, James 1:19-20 warns us to be "slow to speak"; without such control, angry words will spill out, and these do not "bring about the righteous life that God desires." James 1:26 continues, "If anyone considers himself religious and yet does not keep a tight rein on his tongue, he deceives himself and his religion is worthless." Each of us is a case study in the power of Christ to change lives at the very practical level of controlling what we say.

Notice the imagery of James 1:26, of jamming a horse's bit into one's mouth. Philo thinks of the mouth as a dam holding back a raging river. Plutarch reasons that the very nature of the human head demonstrates the need for the tongue to be controlled. Why else, he reasons, is there "a fence of teeth in front of the tongue" and "the brain above it"?

The front line of our spiritual growth, then, is our mouth. The Bible doesn't say we shouldn't talk at all. Rather, our orders are to check and double-check every word that passes.

The Advantages of Control

The primary purpose for controlling our speech is to prevent harm. But controlling our words also has personal advantages for us. The main advantage is that people will respect us.

Just think of how you react differently to a person who goes on and on and talks in circles and one who chooses her words carefully and is succinct. How much respect do you have for the fast-talking used-car salesman, the wisecracking comedian, the politician who speaks out of both sides of his mouth or even the revivalist who enchants crowds with volume and energy? We put people of many words in the category marked "con artists." Now, consider people whom you genuinely respect—perhaps a teacher, a counselor, a grandparent. Aren't they people who speak carefully, using well-chosen words? We put people of few words in the category marked "wise."

Ecclesiastes observes, "The fool multiplies words" (10:14); "A fool is consumed by his own lips" (10:12); "The more the words, the less the meaning" (6:11). Proverbs 17:28 suggests, "Even a fool is thought wise if he keeps silent, and discerning if he holds his tongue." One Jewish rabbi declares that silence is worth twice as much as one word.[1] Philo reports that silence will enhance the effectiveness of our speech.[2] Other rabbis call silence a form of prayer highly valued by God.[3]

Traveling speakers were common in the first-century Greek world.

Plutarch tells two amusing stories about them. He mentions that one day a man named Ephisophon came to Sparta bragging that he could speak the whole day long on any topic someone would suggest. Hearing this, the people ran him out of town, saying, "The good orator must keep his discourse equal to the subject at hand."[4] He also tells of a time when someone praised a traveling orator for his ability to speak much about small matters. Someone nearby quipped, "A shoemaker is not a good craftsman who puts big shoes on small feet."[5] Plutarch himself is fond of pointing out wisdom we should learn from nature. He remarks that geese, in fear of eagles, put stones in their mouths to keep themselves from gaggling when they cross Mt. Taurus.[6]

Aristophanes invented an adjective to describe people who take pride in their ability to talk. He calls them "bambasiloquent,"[7] combining three Greek words to give both an oral and a visual effect. The words on their own mean "pompous," "bundle" and "words." So such a person is a pompous bundle of words. Wrongly, he thinks words are wisdom, and the more words he speaks, the more respect people will have for him. He misunderstands, as we often do, that wisdom requires thoughtful silence and judicious use of words.

Have you ever thought you were offering someone a compliment but they took offense instead? Then you tried to explain what you really meant, only to make matters worse. Every word you spoke seemed to add fuel to the fire. More words didn't help. Finally you realized that "I'm sorry" is really what was needed in the first place.

Perhaps you have embarrassed yourself by trying to explain a joke. As you tried to explain it, you only made it more and more obvious that either it was a bad joke or you did a bad job telling it.

People will respect you if you control your speech. They will think twice about what you have to say. They will value your ideas and counsel because you never speak lightly. They will be interested in your Christian way of life because you have earned their respect.

This leads to a second advantage of controlling our speech. God will use you in special ways if you control your speech. Many biblical examples can be given.

Despite the fact that Moses refers to himself as "slow of speech and tongue" (Ex 4:10), God prefers to work through thick-tongued Moses rather than silver-tongued Aaron. To reassure Moses, God agrees to use Aaron as Moses' mouthpiece. But God knows that now not only will he have to give words to Moses, but he will also have to keep Aaron in check so that he says nothing more than he is supposed to.

In Job, it is not Eliphaz, nor Bildad, nor Zophar, nor even Job who speaks with wisdom, despite the fact that each of Job's friends has three speeches and Job has nine. No, it is Elihu, the young man who has listened patiently to their foolishness, whom God uses to speak with astute wisdom to the situation of Job's misery and the righteousness of God (Job 32—37).

Paul could be long-winded. While in Troas talking to believers, he "kept on talking until midnight" (Acts 20:7). Even after Eutychus fell from a window three floors to his death and Paul brought him back to life, he continued "talking until daylight" (v. 11). However, when Paul was offered the opportunity to present the claims of Christianity to a meeting of the Areopagus (Acts 17:22-31), he delivered a crisp, poignant, challenging speech that keyed in on an altar "to an unknown God." Paul was wise enough to know that the Athenian intellectuals were not going to listen to drivel. Many consider his "Mars Hill" speech the finest presentation of the gospel ever. A big part of its attraction is that the words are carefully chosen, and it is short. We should learn from this.

Paul's opportunity to influence or convert a future Plato or Aristotle was a little like what it would be for you or me to be given a few minutes to speak of the Christian faith on *Donahue* or the *Oprah Winfrey Show*. If you couldn't get to the point quickly, the host would become distracted or cut you off for a commercial. Maybe you have seen Christian entertainers interviewed on the *Tonight Show* or *Late Night with David Letterman*. Sometimes I go away shaking my head, wondering if they have made the best of this fantastic opportunity God has provided them. Yet I must question myself. How would *I* present the gospel in thirty seconds? Could I do any better?

If you and I can learn to be precise in our words, God can use us to his advantage. Especially in these times of video-shortened attention spans and sound bites, we need to learn how to be brief. So when God gives us an opening to speak in his name, we must be alert and focused. We must sharpen our minds and our words. If we cannot, opportunities to speak to our world about the life-changing truth of Christianity will be few.

The New Testament teaches that quietness should be an observable trait in Christians. First Thessalonians 4:11 says, "Make it your ambition to lead a quiet life." "Quiet" does not mean speechless; however, it does mean careful control over our words and an attitude of respect toward others. In fact, the following verse goes on to say that the purpose for this principle of calm is "so that your daily life may win the respect of outsiders." Paul wants non-Christians to think well of Christians, even if they do not agree with our beliefs. The key is for us to control our tongues and esteem others. Today we call this "friendship evangelism." Perhaps our acquaintances will be attracted to Christianity by our demeanor and give us opportunity to speak more directly. But even if not, Christianity is better off for our quietness.

First Timothy 2:2-4 also urges us to "live peaceful and quiet lives"; God delights in this because he "wants all . . . to be saved and to come to a knowledge of the truth." A composed Christian will attract people to the truth claims of Christianity. Is this surprising? Don't we usually picture an evangelistic Christian as aggressive and confrontational? Maybe people have made you feel guilty in the past as they have tried to convince you to do door-to-door evangelism. These passages tell us that a moderate, respectful lifestyle is indeed evangelistic and highly valued by God. However, we must be prepared when the opportunity comes to speak boldly about Christianity.

At numerous points in the New Testament, practical advice demonstrates this motivation of quiet evangelism. Christian slaves, in relating to their masters, are "not to talk back to them . . . so that in every way they will make the teaching about God our Savior attractive" (Tit 2:9-10). Christian wives are to be especially respectful to their non-Christian husbands so that these may be "won over without words" (1 Peter 3:1). Those with the gift of tongues are told by Paul in 1 Corinthians 14 to control it in public worship, for fear of putting off inquisitive visitors who would conclude that Christians are crazy. Paul's injunction for women to control their speaking during public worship, similarly, seems motivated by a concern for putting off non-Christians. In 1 Corinthians 14:35, he speaks of disgrace when he asks women to save their questions until they are home. In 1 Timothy 2:15, he cites "propriety" as a reason for women not to teach in the church.

Maybe you never thought about how you appear to others in your workplace. Yet if people have any inkling that you are a Christian, they are gaining impressions of Christianity by the way you conduct yourself, especially your talk. How do you talk to those you supervise? Do you treat them with respect and understanding? Are they being drawn to Christianity by your composed manner? How about those above you? Do you treat them with respect when you talk to them? How about when you talk to coworkers about your boss? Maybe that's the real test.

Most "unequally yoked" wives I have seen in the church know full well from experience that they cannot browbeat their husbands into the kingdom. It is no accident that such women often develop into the most spiritually mature people in their churches. Their keen desire to win their husbands by quiet evangelism reaps spiritual benefits in them, whether they end up attracting their husbands to Christ or not. We all should learn from this. God is at work in us and through us when we control our talk.

The hope is that quiet evangelism will bring people into a relationship with Christ. However, there is no guarantee. In fact, the New Testament assumes that some will take advantage of this Christian spirit and treat Christians with disdain. Maybe you have experienced this yourself, as I have. Nevertheless, the New Testament encourages us to maintain this kind of witness.

It is even more critical to be calm and respectful amidst persecution. This is the true test. These are moments of opportunity. These are times when the stakes are high and the credibility of Christianity can be demonstrated unmistakably to those around us—who knows which ones will be touched? Even if no one is drawn to Christ by our quiet endurance of humiliation, God is still pleased and will reward us with deepening spiritual character.

First Peter 2:20 says, "But if you suffer for doing good and you endure it, this is commendable before God." Peter goes on to state that God calls us to this purpose and we should never feel that God is asking too much of us. When we suffer quietly for our Christian commitment, we are following in the example of someone who had much more reason to complain than we do. Peter quotes Isaiah 53:9 to establish that unlike you and me, Christ was sinless when he was tortured, abused and crucified. Nevertheless, he was quiet through this ordeal and through his unjust trial, as the Gospels emphasize (Mt 26:63; Mk 14:61; Lk 23:9; Jn 18:9). "When he suffered, he made no threats," says 1 Peter 2:23. Rather, he looked to God with confidence that his Father would be pleased. Jesus' prayer at Gethsemane for this cup of suffering to pass shows that he did not desire to suffer for good any more than we do (Mt 26:36-46; Mk 14:32-42; Lk 22:41-46). He suffered because he was good, the unblemished sacrifice. He "bore our sins in his body," as 1 Peter 2:24 says. However, because he did suffer on our behalf, the ultimate spiritual blessing was obtained for the world. "By his wounds, you have been healed" (1 Pet 2:24). Everyone now may come to God clean through Christ.

Jesus Christ is the ultimate example of how God accomplishes his will and extends his kingdom through those who control their words. When we develop a peaceful spirit that people can observe by our tempered talk, God can accomplish limitless things through us. If we want God to use us, we had better begin controlling our speech today.

Where to Begin Controlling Our Tongues

Obviously, we cannot be silent all the time. Conversation with others is basic to being human. God gave us the gift of speech, and we should use it in our ongoing relationships with others. However, we must also value control. I hope that what you have read so far has motivated you to implement control into your talk. Still, you may have the impression that control is only for special spiritual situations. Nothing could be further from the truth. Controlling words is valuable in any situation. But it makes sense to begin efforts to control our speech at the most mundane levels. After accomplishing control in these areas, we can work our way toward dealing with more difficult situations.

Think of it like learning any new skill, whether it be a sport like baseball or a personal skill like using a computer. We begin with the fundamentals, like how to throw and catch or how to enter and exit DOS. After mastering these basics, we move on to playing the game with squeeze bunts and double steals or stringing macro commands and learning Fortran.

A good place to begin efforts to control our speech is at the level of politeness. For example, it is rude to interrupt others when they are talking. At our house, we constantly remind our children to wait to talk until others finish. It is not easy for them, because they're afraid they will forget what they wanted to say. Sometimes my wife and I are not much better than they are. Yet we must be willing to risk not having the opportunity to speak at all out of respect for others. It may well be that the conversation will turn another direction and our two cents will no longer be relevant. So what? Will the earth stop turning if our precious words are never uttered?

Perhaps you have done what I do sometimes. What I want to say is at the tip of my tongue. While the other person is talking I lean forward, ready to jump into the conversation. Sensing that she is about finished, I pounce, practically making my first word a compound with her last word. This tactic applies the letter of basic speech ethics but not the spirit. I have shown that I am not at all interested in what the other person is saying. I just want to talk. Really, I am still interrupting when I do this. Halting such below-the-belt conversational tactics is fundamental speech ethics.

Sound advice along these lines comes from 'Abot, one of the oldest written collections of rabbinic sayings. It is every bit as good as Miss Manners or Ann Landers. 'Abot 5:10 says,

A wise man does not speak ahead of him who is greater than he is in wisdom and does not interrupt the speech of his associate. He is not hasty to answer. He questions according to the subject matter and answers to the point. He speaks about the first thing first and the last thing last. Regarding that which he does not know, he says, "I do not know." He acknowledges the truth. The reverse of this is to be found in the boor.

We do ourselves and Christ no good if we cannot apply the most primary conventions of social etiquette in our conversation. Psalm 32:9 warns us, "Do not be like the horse or the mule, which have no understanding." This is a good place to begin speech control. Let's stop being mules!

A second basic area in which to begin applying speech control is in explaining something to someone. Simply, try to explain things with fewer words. Get to the point! Respect the patience and interest of those listening. This is the other side of the coin of not interrupting. Give others time to respond.

Teachers and preachers are notorious for waxing eloquent, taking advantage of captive audiences. This is why clocks are always at the rear of the sanctuary, to remind the preacher not to go past noon! Long-time Christians are all too aware that most sermons are too long and would affect us more if they were shorter. I mention this not to put down preachers, but to help you realize that almost everything you say, too, could be said with considerably fewer words and also be more potent. Even as I write this, I'm aware that my editor will dispose of a number words on this page, to help you respond better to the ideas I am trying to get across.

Proverbs 18:4 expresses this concept by contrasting different types of water: "The words of a man's mouth are deep waters, but the fountain of wisdom is a bubbling brook." The phrase "deep waters" should be taken negatively, as in Proverbs 20:5, conveying the idea of unfathomable obscurity. When we use too many words to get something across, we muddy the waters and no one can see the point. The phrase "bubbling brook" may give you the wrong impression, since "bubbling" sounds like lots of talk to us. Actually, here the word helps picture a fresh, clear, invigorating stream. Simple, carefully chosen words make our ideas easy to see.

The Greek moralist Plutarch gives the following secondhand drama review: "It seems to have been Melanthius who, being asked about Diogenes' tragedy, said he could not get sight of it, there were so many words in the way."[8] I guess such a comment would parallel the common complaint "I can't see the forest for the trees." Let's begin, then, by simply cutting down on our words in everyday conversation.

My final suggestion about where to begin speech control involves the people we talk to. Limiting our conversation with certain people is good, basic speech ethics. I'm sure you have experienced situations where nothing you say seems to penetrate into someone's awareness. We say, "It's like water running off a duck's back." Sirach 21:14 suggests that it's more like pouring water into a broken jar. In such cases we sense that our words are wasted and ineffective. Maybe the person is simply not very bright; maybe he or she is just not interested in what we are talking about. Regardless, it is pointless to keep talking, and we should learn to quit.

A striking example of this is the story of the paralyzed man who is carried to Jesus by his friends (Mt 9:1-8). When Jesus says, "Take heart, son; your sins are forgiven," the scribes grumble that his audacity constitutes blasphemy. Jesus informs them that he knows their evil thoughts. He realizes that the lesson on forgiveness he intended to demonstrate with this young man is lost on them. Because of their closed minds and hearts, he cuts off his efforts to explain. With a seeming wave of his hand in disappointment, he heals the young man: "Get up, take your mat and go home."

In Matthew 7:6, Jesus exhorts us with the principle behind such action. He says, "Do not give dogs what is sacred; do not throw your pearls to pigs." What we are saying becomes devalued when we offer it to those who treat it with disdain. Dogs are not capable of reverently handling the bread and the wine of Communion. Pigs cannot attend a gala with pearls around their necks.

In the Jewish context of this saying, it is even worse than this. Dogs were not pets but wild animals that roamed in packs, feeding off garbage and terrorizing villages. Pigs were dirty, unfit to eat and often wild also. Jesus goes on to say, then, that certain people not only will treat our offering with disgust but may also "turn and tear [us] to pieces." People can become violent when we tell them things they don't want to hear, whether this be the gospel, some kind of advice or even a fact that we find interesting. We must learn to walk away and leave them alone sometimes. We can wait for more opportune moments.

Sirach 37:11 notes nine topics inappropriate to discuss with certain types of people—for example, it is wrong to talk to a lazy man about work, to a cruel man about mercy, to a coward about war and to a woman about her rival. You get the idea. I'm sure we could make up an endless list like this. The point is if what you say has merit, save it for a receptive audience. Don't present it to people who couldn't care less. When you detect their hostility or simple lack of interest, stop yourself from continuing to talk. This is basic speech ethics.

The matter of the people we talk to has a second prong. We should also consider whom we choose to spend our time with. Our speech can be infected by our association with people who do not control their speech. Their bad speech habits will rub off on us. If we spend time with people who gossip, we will gossip also. If we pal around with people who get kicks out of making fun of others, we will find ourselves enjoying this kind of sinful speech too. Every parent knows this. We work hard to monitor our children's friends. We try to get to know their friends, and sometimes discourage certain friendships. It makes sense to apply this principle to ourselves as well as we begin to work on our speech ethics.

In this light, Proverbs 24:1-2 warns,

Do not envy wicked men,
> do not desire their company;
for their hearts plot violence,
> and their lips talk about making trouble.

Sirach 22:12 advises, "Speak seldom with the stupid man, be not the companion of a brute." Let's face squarely the bad influences in our lives and determine to control the amount of time we spend with them.

The Impossibility of Complete Control

This chapter's purpose is to move you forward into a Christian lifestyle that implements basic speech ethics. But let's be honest. There is only so much we can do. Our tongue is a powerful force for evil and can outmaneuver us over and over again. How many times have you determined not to shout at your children, only to do so moments later? How many times have you said, "I shouldn't say this, but . . ."? How many times have you desired to greet a stranger at church but walked on by?

The Bible does not hedge regarding the power of the tongue, and we shouldn't either. Psalm 52:4 chastises the human tongue as if it were a person: "You love every harmful word, O you deceitful tongue!" Proverbs

6:2 pictures our own tongues turning and trapping us so that they can master us. Ecclesiastes 10:12 pictures lips as cannibals, smacking with delight as they stand over their human victim, a person "consumed by his own lips." Proverbs 12:6 says that like vampires, words can "lie in wait for blood," and Proverbs 19:28 says they "gulp down evil."

One particular image in the Bible makes it clear that the tongue's evil is not from itself but from an internal source. Psalm 59:7 says the evil tongue belches ("spew" in NIV) swords; Proverbs 15:28 says it belches ("gushes") evil. As gross as this image is, it conveys a critical truth. Obviously, our tongue itself is not the problem; neither are our lips and mouth. These only represent the problem of sin that comes from within us. It is this evil nature of ours that we must overcome in order to control our speech. Jesus says in Matthew 15:18-19, "But the things that come out of the mouth come from the heart, and these make a man 'unclean.' For out of the heart come evil thoughts, murder, adultery, sexual immorality, theft, false testimony, slander."

James 3:1-13 elaborates on the problem of the tongue. It is the most extensive treatment in the New Testament, and it does not draw a very pretty picture. In fact, this passage is more negative than anything else written in the Bible or other literature of the day. Here James intends to discourage the overly ambitious and immature from aspiring to be teachers in the church. Indeed, anyone who reads this passage carefully should be mortified.

In verse 6 James calls the tongue "a fire" and proceeds to list four aspects of its destructive nature. First, he says that the tongue "is appointed a world of evil among the parts of the body" (my translation). The passive verb here presumes that the one who tapped the tongue for this role of mob boss of the body is God. The tongue's role as the central distribution point for our evil is beyond its capacity to change, or ours. God made us this way.

Although most modern Bible translations have "is" rather than "is appointed," I assure you that verse 6 does contain the Greek verb "appoint."[9] Actually, the form of the verb here could be passive or middle. A middle sense would be reflexive, meaning that the tongue appoints itself, like a South American rebel overthrowing the government and declaring himself dictator. However, earlier images of the tongue as a rudder or bit in verses 3-4 support the concept of the tongue not as an independent power but as a tool of others. Further, verse 12 drives home the point that the tongue cannot change its evil ways, any more than a fig tree can become an olive tree or a salt spring a fresh spring. This is its natural, created identity.

Second, in verse 6 James says that the tongue "corrupts the whole person." Often in the New Testament the Greek word translated "person" here refers to a person's physical body. It can, as it does here, refer to a person in all aspects—mental, emotional, spiritual, physical. The Greek word translated "corrupts" specifically refers to ruining clothes by spilling something on them that stains. So picture the tongue as an inkwell that stains the entire body, inside and out. It stains us with a corruption that we cannot ever wash off. Like Lady Macbeth, we may wash over and over with no effect. The tongue ruins us—and makes our ruin obvious to everyone.

Third, verse 6 says that the tongue "sets the whole course of his life on fire." James employs the fire metaphor to describe the tongue's ever-widening sphere of destruction. The phrase "the whole course of his life" is tricky. Translating it into English involves much more than just substituting words. A literal translation would be "wheel of birth." In Greek culture, the phrase was used to depict the ongoing difficulties of coping with life, perhaps something like "fate" in the pessimistic, Shakespearean sense. "Wheel of birth" attempts to express that life is bigger than I am. I am only a small cog in the machinations of society.

The NIV translation quoted above is unfortunate because it restricts the concept to one individual. James has already described the tongue's devastation of the whole individual in the second phrase. So when James says that our tongues torch this "wheel of birth," he means that the tongue devastates an entire society. It does much more than corrupt a person. Collectively, our tongues bring down the whole world of humanity with us. The idea parallels the image of a spark destroying a forest which James provides at the end of verse 5. My tongue doesn't just ruin me, it ruins everyone around me. Human tongues make human life bad.

The fourth point about the human tongue in James 3:6 is that it "is itself set on fire by hell." This is not an image of the tongue's destruction. Rather, it conveys that the source of the tongue's capability to devastate people and society is hell. The Greek word for "hell" in the Septuagint translates a Hebrew word used in 2 Kings 23:10 and Jeremiah 7:31 to refer to places of burning for pagan fire sacrifices. Later it was used to refer to a constantly burning garbage dump outside the walls of Jerusalem. Today we still picture Satan working out of a cavern of flames below the earth. Our tongues, then, are minions of Satan. Satan gains access to our lives through our tongues in order to destroy us and to destroy people around us.

If verse 6 is not enough to make us feel helpless against the evils of our tongues, James goes on in verses 7-8 to contrast the tongue with all the animals that humankind is able to dominate. We can capture and train them, but the tongue does not bend to our will. It resists all our efforts to tame it. It is wild. James adds the picture of the tongue being like a snake, striking with deadly poison.

In verses 9-10 James expresses his dismay at the fact that this same instrument of evil is employed to praise God. When we use it to honor God, we employ it for its highest purpose. It seems almost sacrilegious to use something so defiled and opposed to God in this way, but it is all we have. James seems to be shaking his head in despondency when he says in verse 10, "This should not be."

Indeed it should not be, but it is. However, at the beginning of this passage exposing the tongue's evil nature, verse 2 acknowledges that the evil of our tongues is a component of our sinful nature. If some ideal person could keep the tongue perfectly controlled, he could also "keep his whole body in check." Of course James knows, as you and I know from experience, that we can never completely control our words, any more than we can stop sinning.

As pointed out earlier, James paints a very dark picture because he wants to discourage people from being eager to teach in the church. Yet he desires qualified people to be teachers. So he assumes that a qualitative difference exists between various Christians' ability to control their tongues. Concentration on controlling our tongues is a basic aspect of our growing in spiritual maturity.

Damage Control

Today we speak of the need for "damage control" when a politician's image is threatened by embarrassing leaks to the press or when a big company's stock is plummeting because of bad decisions. When a fire rages for weeks at a national forest, the firefighters know the most they can hope to do is limit the destruction, so they dig trenches and ignite backfires.

Damage control is what we must apply to our tongues. We can't hope to stop the harm it causes. However, we can dig trenches. We can decrease its range. We can box it in. We can hold it down. If we desire to grow in our Christian lives, this is the place to begin real change.

We will not gain much control over this powerful force in our lives without access to a mightier power. Although James does not specify what this is, Psalm 141:3 poignantly supplicates God: "Set a guard over my mouth, O LORD; keep watch over the door of my lips."

Let's put this verse on the refrigerator or the bathroom mirror. Make it our daily prayer.

5

A Vital Bridge

Listening

*M*ost of us don't like to draw attention to our ears. They're cute on babies and essential to hang our glasses on, but they are not a prized feature of our appearance. They are too big or too little; some are bent, and all are crinkly. We laugh at the ears of elephants and donkeys, but when we take time to look at the ears stuck on the sides of our own heads, they're pretty funny too.

If we rated how we value our senses, hearing might run a dead heat with smell, but I have a feeling both would run far behind sight. In this chapter, for once, our ears and their capacity to listen will be on center stage. The reason is that listening is absolutely essential to the ethics of talk. It is the bridge that spans the control of talk and actually talking.

If you have taken to heart the challenge of chapter four to reduce your talking, you are going to be left with some empty space. What are you going to do with all that extra time when you are no longer talking? In this chapter I want to invite you to spend that time listening. Listening is the very best thing you can do to prepare yourself for opportunities to talk.

Ears are like bridges in more ways than one. We don't think much about bridges unless they are not there. Living in the St. Louis area in the summer of 1993, I watched countless bridges washed away by the flooding Mississippi. The result was that the normal functions of community life came to a halt. Think about how loss of hearing would affect your life. It would not stop your body from functioning, but could you do your job? Wouldn't it diminish the entertainment value of a movie or television? What about the music you enjoy? Could you even play tennis?

I certainly can't speak for those who cope with deafness. However, as I imagine it, the worst aspect of becoming deaf would be the sense of detachment from other people. Even though I could still talk, conversation with others would require a great deal of effort that I expect could become extremely frustrating. Would I feel so out of sync with others that I would quit trying to converse? I don't know.

This is why I call listening a bridge. It is vital to communication, just as a bridge is vital to travel. When a bridge is gone, relationships between people on either side of the river stop. When hearing goes, meaningful talk is hindered.

Why We Should Listen

Our ability to speak well depends on our ability to listen well. It is really as simple as that. An ancient Egyptian proverb says, "When hearing is good, speaking is good."[1] We know this to be true from our own experience. Whether we are responding in a formal debate or talking with our two-year-old, we must listen intently before we talk. If we don't, what we say doesn't connect. It is wasted.

According to Proverbs 18:13, talking without listening goes beyond wasted communication. It reflects poorly on us in at least two ways. To do this, it says, is a person's "folly and his shame."

How does speaking without listening shame us? Well, how do we feel when we address someone we just met as Elizabeth when her name is Jennifer? How do we feel about yelling at our spouse for bothering us when they just wanted to ask if they could help? How do we feel when we ask a question that the instructor has just answered? Don't we feel embarrassed? We want to crawl under a rock. We apologize profusely, even though the damage has been done. If only we had listened before speaking.

James 1:19 contains a three-part proverb that relates to this: "Everyone should be quick to listen, slow to speak and slow to become angry." The word *everyone* tells us that this is a universal observation that applies to all of us in many, varied circumstances. Like many proverbs, this one is not explained in its context. We are left to ponder its obvious truth. All three parts of the proverb are worthy admonitions on their own, but what is the intention of stringing them together?

The three-part proverb contains a progression that begins with listening. Attentive listening results in judicious speaking, which in turn curtails angry speech. Control of speech and anger depends on listening. Angry speech here represents many kinds of sinful speech, particularly those we regret. Such words shame us because they come out before we catch them.

Christian writer Walter Wangerin describes a time when he humiliated himself because of anger.[2] When he and his wife, Thanne, would fight, at first he "did the talking" and "she did the not-talking." After some crying from her and bullying from him, she would blurt out "an ocean of wrongs, such a delineation of sin in such numbered and dated detail" that he would leave their apartment and walk the sidewalks for three hours at a time. On one such wintry night he slammed the tail of his coat in the locked apartment door, leaving the keys inside. Now he could choose to freeze without his coat or knock meekly on the door. He knocked on the door. Seeing his predicament, Thanne began laughing—a genuine, sweet laugh of forgiveness she thought he would share. "But what did the dummy do?" asks Wangerin. He left in angry, stupid disgrace.

He did not hear her cries of unhappiness. He did not hear her laughter of forgiveness. And so he humiliated himself by what he said and did.

Each of us could relate a story of our own like this, because we aren't quick to hear often enough. But we can develop the willingness to listen. It's a matter of concentration and concern. It needs to become a spiritual priority.

We're aware of how not listening can lead to shame. How can it make us appear foolish? The idea here is that not listening makes what we say ignorant and uninformed. The Old Testament says many things about fools, but one that is repeated over and over is that the fool doesn't listen. In contrast to the wise, the fool doesn't heed instruction (Prov 12:15; 13:13) or listen to rebuke (Prov 13:1). He doesn't obey authority (Prov 10:8).

I don't know about you, but when I hear someone—a guest on a talk show, a politician, a teacher or even a preacher—say something I know to be incorrect, my tendency is to question everything else that person says. People who speak need to be well informed about their subject. Certainly this is true in the public sphere, but it is equally true in private conversations. If we want people to respect us, we had better be informed.

Listening makes us informed. It makes us wise. Proverbs 19:20 counsels, "Listen to advice and accept instruction, and in the end you will be wise," and Proverbs 15:31 says, "He who listens to a life-giving rebuke will be at home among the wise." In Proverbs 5:1-2, Wisdom herself invites:

My son, pay attention to my wisdom,
　listen well to my words of insight,
that you may maintain discretion
　and your lips may preserve knowledge.

The verb phrases "pay attention" and "listen well" underline that obtaining wisdom requires effort on our part. Concentration, as the first verb requires, is difficult. How many times do you lose concentration during a twenty-minute sermon? How easily do you get distracted when your spouse is trying to tell you something *important?* Concentration takes work and practice. In Hebrew the verb "listen well" pictures us stretching out our ears to hear. Obviously we don't do this literally, but when we are concentrating to hear and understand someone, it is as if we mentally enlarge our ears. The point is that we must initiate and maintain effort to grow in wisdom through listening to others. Well-informed speech will result.

One of the things that can divert us the most from good listening is talking. When we are talking, we cannot listen well. This is not just a matter of concentration. Mostly it's simple biology. We only have so much hearing capacity. When we speak, a great deal of this capacity is taken up with the sound of our own voice, leaving little room for hearing anything else. To try to listen and speak at the same time creates an overload. The Greek moralist Plutarch says we should listen twice as much as we talk: that is why we have two ears and one mouth.[3] In disdain, he also says, "While others retain what is said, in nonstop talkers it goes straight through in a flux; they then go around like empty containers, void of wisdom, but full of noise."[4]

Let's not be "empty containers" but rather fill ourselves with all the wisdom that is available to us. Let's listen twice as much as we talk, or at least more than we talk. This is no game. Much is at stake in our spiritual vitality.

What It Means to Listen

I can order my ten-year-old to listen to me all I want. I can raise my voice. I can hold him directly in front of me. I can make him look me in the eye. Although these things may have some effect, I cannot *force* him to listen. Listening is something that takes place inside him. He can slam shut the lead door between his ears and that place anytime he wants to. He can also open the lead door to varying degrees. It is when he decides to leave it open all the way that I really enjoy talking to him. Then he wants to hear me and is using all his faculties to ingest and understand what I am saying. And he will respond with wisdom and integrity.

His lead door is not completely shut too often right now, but I imagine that a few years from now it will be shut a great deal. In growing out of adolescence, we should gain increasing capacity to open that door further and learn to hear others well. This is a spiritual quest for us all.

But what is behind the inner lead door? Where do the words go when we are really listening? I don't know if that mystery can be completely solved, but the Bible consistently refers to our hearts as the place where words go when truly heard. Proverbs 4:20-21 equates listening "closely to my words" with keeping them "within your heart." Proverbs 22:17 relates paying attention with applying to our hearts what is taught.

Jeremiah 7:26 refers to Israel as "stiff-necked" because "they did not listen" or "pay attention" to God—they did not allow his word to get to their hearts. Perhaps the image is that they blocked the passageway from the ears to the heart. This is where the lead door is closed. Probably it also means that they would not turn their head to "incline their ears" toward God. They looked straight ahead, ignoring him.

Greek writers like Plutarch tend to speak of the soul rather than the heart as the place of true listening. He speaks of "the babbler's ears" as having "no passage bored through to the soul."[5] Whether we call it our heart, our soul or our mind, there is a part of ourselves that defines and encompasses who we really are and what we really think. It is certainly beyond our physical parts, beyond even our mental and emotional capacities. It's the essential us, the us that continues into eternity, whether with God or apart from God. These other things are instruments of who we are. When we truly listen, what we have heard becomes a part of us. It becomes assimilated into who we now are. Something said to us that we have not truly heard remains outside of us. It does not penetrate our being.

The true demonstration of what we have heard is our life itself. This is why Plutarch can say, "Right listening is the beginning of right living."[6] It is also why the Bible so often associates listening with obedience. Proverbs 6:20 says, "My son, keep your father's commands and do not forsake your mother's teaching." Through Jeremiah, God proclaims to Israel, "When I brought your forefathers out of Egypt, . . . I gave them this command: Obey me. . . . But they did not listen or pay attention; instead, they followed the stubborn inclinations of their evil hearts" (Jer 7:22-24).

In Ezekiel 33:32, God compares Israel's response to Ezekiel's message with the way we respond to entertainment—we listen and enjoy, but we do not act on it. To Ezekiel he says, "To them you are nothing more than one who sings love songs . . . for they hear your words but do not put them into practice."

Jeremiah 31:33-34 anticipates a time when God will radically simplify the process of obedience. He will cut out the need for listening and go straight for the heart. "I will put my law in their minds and write it on their hearts," he says. Who we are will be entirely consistent with what God desires. No separation, no lead door, will exist.

With God's Spirit in our lives, the capacity for such union with God's own heart exists now, and we need to tap into it. We must listen. We must open the doorway to who we are so that we may learn and grow, so that when we speak we may have something worth hearing.

Who to Listen To

On her 1985 *Unguarded* album, Amy Grant sings a song entitled "Who to Listen To." The haunting refrain echoes, "You know they're going to hit you from all sides; better make up your mind who to, who not to listen to." It dramatizes that many voices compete for our attention. We must make hundreds of decisions daily regarding which ones we open the door to. The song underlines also that these are spiritually formative choices: "You've got to know there is a bigger plan. . . . Pray for the plan to begin in you."

Who are we supposed to listen to? When seeking advice, millions of people write to "Dear Abby" or Ann Landers. Some call those astrology 900 numbers. What do you do? Who do you listen to?

Just like me, you listen to people you trust: your parents, your spouse, a friend, a teacher, a minister. There may be a newscaster you respect, like Ted Koppel, or a columnist, like Bob Greene, and maybe an author, like James Dobson or Billy Graham. Why do you listen to these people? Because they have proved reliable. You have found their ideas, their advice, to be true.

Who *don't* we listen to? Maybe the same people sometimes. Mostly, however, we have turned off people who have shown themselves unreliable—maybe a friend who lied to us or an authority whose ideas have been proved false. Just think about the many diet plans you have tried and found wanting.

Is there a bigger plan we are supposed to relate to in all this, as Amy Grant sings? Certainly. Let's consult the Bible for help.

I have already quoted from Proverbs 6:20, which emphasizes listening to our parents. Verse 21 goes on to encourage us to retain their words of counsel like strings of pearls: "Fasten them around your neck." Our parents' words are valuable, but we need them close at hand if we're to use them every day.

When you walk, they will guide you;
> when you sleep, they will watch over you;
> when you awake, they will speak to you. (v. 22)

So much of who we are comes from our parents, or others who raised us. Occasionally we recognize a parent's voice surging out of us as we correct or advise our children or explain to our spouse our reasoning for something we do.

I tend to hesitate to invite our children's friends into our house to play. When my wife asked me about this, I remembered that my parents often counseled me against inviting my playmates to our home, because they thought it invited trouble. As I think about it, their position was probably a precaution because they often were not home after school. They trusted me in our house, but not my friends. My wife's experience was the opposite, and she often invites children in.

There is also the humorous story about one family's practice of always cutting the end off a ham before they put it in the oven. When the husband asked his wife why she did this, she responded, "Because my mother always did." When her mother was asked why she cut off the end of the ham before roasting it, she said the same thing. Finally the grandmother, when asked, recalled that she began doing this because the only roasting pan she owned was too small for a ham.

Much of what our parents have taught us is so tightly ingrained in who we are that we couldn't sort it out if we tried. But that is true learning, as I have just described it, and is probably what the proverb has in mind too. Now, everything we have gained from our parents like this is not necessarily good. Perhaps we were verbally abused as a child and are now carrying out the same drubbing on our own children, in a perverse way thinking this is normal. But sorting out and identifying the valuable things our parents have instilled in us is healthy and good. For the most part and for most of us, we can trust their advice still, and we should.

In Job 8:8, Bildad goes beyond parents in advising us who to listen to. He recommends that we "ask the former generations and find out what their fathers learned." Whether we are seeking advice on how to discipline our children or preparing a Bible study on Revelation 20, it is always valuable to gain a perspective from history and tradition. Human wisdom on any subject builds from one generation to another. Trusting information that ignores this tradition is extremely risky. We usually label such stuff "off the wall."

This is not to say we should be stuck in the past. Rather, it is to say that the past always has something to teach us. If contemporary understanding is not informed by the past, it is foolish. Usually we should avoid people who peddle their ideas as "new and completely different" and seek people whose ideas build on tradition.

When Proverbs 22:17 encourages us to "pay attention and listen to the sayings of the wise," this is exactly what it has in mind. The "sayings of the wise" amount to teaching that builds on tradition. It sorts out the good and bad of tradition through experience and continued observation. People who do this are worth listening to. Included in this category may be a stimulating teacher or writer in an area of your interest. We are good stewards of our time and our life when we determine to make room for such people to influence us.

The Bible operates on the basis that wisdom comes from two directions: vertical and horizontal. Both come from God, but they employ different routes and different mediums to reach us. Vertical wisdom comes directly from God through the Bible, prayer and sometimes preaching. It corresponds to the voice of the prophet in the Old Testament, which we recognize as the source of God's word immediately. Horizontal wisdom is not so direct. Its package isn't labeled "from God." It might say, "From Shakespeare" or "From *U.S. News and World Report.*" It corresponds to the kind of wisdom we see in Proverbs and Ecclesiastes.

Listening to tradition and parents is seeking God's wisdom in the horizontal plane. God created the whole world, and all that is good and true—including ideas—comes from him. Too many of us tend to limit our hunt for God's wisdom to the vertical. But the Bible itself, our chief source of vertical wisdom, urges us to seek beyond its pages to what lies in the horizontal. Proverbs 2:1-6 instructs:

My son, if you accept my words
    and store up my commands within you,

turning your ear to wisdom
and applying your heart to understanding, . . .
and if you look for it as for silver
and search for it as for hidden treasure,
then you will understand the fear of the LORD
and find the knowledge of God.
For the LORD gives wisdom,
and from his mouth come knowledge and understanding.

In the New Testament, Philippians 4:8 advises, "Whatever is true, whatever is noble, whatever is right, whatever is pure, whatever is lovely, whatever is admirable—if anything is excellent or praiseworthy—think about such things."

Our quest, then, is to listen for God's voice wherever we may hear it, including in the horizontal plane that surrounds us daily.

The Bible also encourages us to seek the vertical, more direct path to God's wisdom. We hear this encouragement more in the Psalms and the Prophets. Psalm 119:130 says, "The unfolding of your words gives light." "Teach me your way, O LORD," says Psalm 86:11, "and I will walk in your truth." The command "Hear, O Israel" resounds throughout the Old Testament, from the first command to the last prophet.[7] In Psalm 50:16-19 God warns that to "hate my instruction" is to link arms with thieves and adulterers. As I already pointed out, Israel was judged and punished because the people stopped listening to God.

By the time of Jesus, the practices of rabbis and the people of Qumran reveal that this basic lesson had been learned. In Qumran, the people committed themselves to studying Scripture all day long. Not only did they do this, but they copied and preserved Scripture that we profit from today. Whatever one may say about the Essenes' peculiar ways, their love for Scripture stands out.

Although the rabbis were bitter enemies of those at Qumran, they retained a similar dedication to the study of Scripture. "Be diligent in the study of the Torah!" they advocate.[8] They warn against distractions while studying Scripture and promote the idea that nothing is more valuable. Offered a thousand gold coins, many precious stones and pearls, one should choose study of Scripture instead.[9]

You and I, too, need this kind of dedication to the study of Scripture. It is only there and in prayer that we have direct access to the wisdom of God. So if we desire to listen to God, we must focus on these particular words awaiting our discovery in Scripture. Of course we need to learn how to discover God's word for us and our situation amid the intentions the biblical authors had for their original audiences. We must grapple with the language and cultural gaps and other difficulties. However, this is precisely why a lifetime of regular, diligent study of the Bible is required of us.

The Roman philosopher Seneca tells us we should listen to those who promote virtue.[10] Philo wants us to ignore those who employ flash and glitter to draw us to the trivial, and instead to give keen attention to those who impart truth with quiet composure.[11] The direction and focus of the Bible point to us the one person in whom the wisdom of God and the wisdom of humanity intersect. Jesus rises above all others as someone we should listen to.

In Jesus a unique source of wisdom enters the picture. His words utter vertical and horizontal wisdom simultaneously, for he is both God and man. He encompasses both the prophetic voice and tradition. He *is* the wisdom of God in the flesh. He stands in history as God's Word to humankind. Colossians 2:3 says that in him "are hidden all the treasures of wisdom and knowledge." Is there anyone to whom we should listen more intently than Jesus? Who else will better enable us to sort out the truth of wisdom from the falsehood of foolishness in ourselves and those around us?

Jesus often challenged his audiences, as he does us, with the refrain "He who has ears, let him hear.[12] It is essential that we listen closely to Jesus, because hearing him is not only a matter of our present well-being but also a matter of our eternal life or death. Jesus knows that if we allow his words to penetrate the lead door of our sinful hearts, our relationship with God will be changed radically and eternally. "Whoever who hears my word," Jesus says in John 5:24, ". . . has crossed over from death to life."[13]

In Matthew 11:25 Jesus offers praise to God because he has "hidden these things from the wise and learned, and revealed them to little children." What do "little children" know? They know that the absolutely vital key to knowing God is Jesus. "All things have been committed to me by my Father," he says in 11:27, ". . . and no one knows the Father except the Son and those to whom the Son chooses to reveal him." He completes his thoughts in 11:28-30 by urging those listening to become his disciples and "learn from me."

Paul parallels and extends these thoughts of Jesus in 1 Corinthians 1:18-31, speaking of how the lowly and despised recognize that Jesus is the wisdom of God while the philosophers and holy men miss him altogether. "The foolishness of God is wiser than man's wisdom," he asserts, and for Christians, Jesus is the wisdom from God (vv. 25, 30). This perfect wisdom brings us "righteousness, holiness and redemption." Jesus is the key to life as we live it now and the life we will lead eternally.

Some may question the value of all this, since Jesus is no longer here on earth. As with other wise men who have come and gone across the stage of history, all we have to go on now is a few of Jesus' words, they may say. This, of course, is where Jesus has a distinct advantage over all other voices of wisdom. He is, remember, not just a wise man but the wisdom of God. He died like all others, but through the power of God he also rose from the dead. He lives and provides us twenty-four-hour access to his wisdom. Jesus provides this access by giving us the Holy Spirit. Paul says in 1 Corinthians 2:10-12:

> The Spirit searches all things, even the deep things of God. For who among men knows the thoughts of a man except the man's spirit within him? In the same way no one knows the thoughts of God except the Spirit of God. We have not received the spirit of the world but the Spirit who is from God, that we may understand what God has freely given us.

With the Spirit of Christ in us we are properly equipped to listen and discern the wisdom we need to know.

New Ears

Receiving the Spirit is like receiving a new pair of ears. These new ears will help us decide "who to, who not to listen to." They will also bring our daily decisions into the "bigger plan." Everything we hear, everything we read, everything we watch—all influences on us can be siphoned through our new ears to reveal the true wisdom that is coming to us from God. Whether we are listening to our grandfather or a song on the radio, reading "Peanuts" or a book by Michael Crichton, watching a bad movie or a good television program, studying our Bible or enduring a poor sermon, the Spirit whom Jesus has given us will reveal the true wisdom we need from the throng of voices that compete for our attention.

Of course these new ears of ours won't help much if the lead door to our heart is left closed. We must keep the door open and let the Spirit live there with us. Think of the Holy Spirit as a super Siskel and Ebert. If we let him, he will sit with us on the couch and offer totally reliable critiques not just about movies but about absolutely everything we encounter.

With our new ears and all-knowing Wise Critic in place, we are ready to listen. As we do so, we are crossing the bridge to wise speech and are ready to talk. This will be the subject of the next chapter.

6

Twin Goals

Truth & Grace

*M*y wife and I have twin boys, Gavin and Kyle. Since the day of their birth, we have strived to treat them as equally as possible. As babies they were fed, burped and changed on the same schedule. As children they received their Big Wheels, tricycles, bicycles and baseball gloves on the same days. Neither of them has gotten shirts, shoes, shorts or slacks without the other also getting them. They both participate in band, soccer, baseball, Scouts and camp. When we praise one, we praise the other; when we hug one, we hug the other.

Of course we know they are different. They're fraternal twins, not identical. They don't look, talk or eat alike. One likes to read about horses or BMX racing; the other likes to read fantasy or books about making films. One likes to write stories; the other likes to fix his bike. They have their own friends. They have distinct personalities. They are individuals with their own strengths, weaknesses and potentials.

By the way we relate to them, they know they are equally important to us, even though they know and we know they are unique.

Like twins, truth and grace are equal in their value for speech. Both are essential, yet they are very different. We need to draw upon both when we talk, but we must not favor one over the other. If we don't balance truth with grace, we may be right but uncaring. If we are heavy on grace, what we say may be sweet, but it will lack substance.

This chapter will discuss the importance of both truth and grace in our speech. It will describe what truth and grace are, how we obtain them and how we use them when we talk. You can bet after what I just said that I will strive to give them equal treatment.

This chapter brings us to the heart and soul of this book. We are now talking about how to talk. Chapter one demonstrated how powerful speech can be; chapters two and three detailed what not to say; chapters four and five covered matters preliminary to speaking: having the upper hand over our mouths and learning what is going on before we speak. So at last we have come to the matter of what we are going to say. What should be the content of our talk from a biblical perspective?

Gracious Talk

Some people are a joy to be around. Spending time with them makes us feel good about ourselves. We look forward to every opportunity to be with them. If we think about it, we realize that what draws us to these favorite people has a lot to do with what they say to us. They encourage; they inform; they challenge; they love; they forgive, they help; they smile.

Many people who attract us like this will be friends of ours, but some are mere acquaintances. Do you ever switch lines at the supermarket when you recognize a checker who is usually pleasant to you? Isn't it true that something as simple as the friendly manner of a teller at the bank can make you feel better after an otherwise disastrous day? Doesn't a cheery waitress or waiter improve dinner?

Gracious talk increases the quality of our lives. Without it, depression and despair reign. Gracious talk is courteous, kind, helpful, articulate and gentle. It seeks the best for others. It cares.

Notice that gracious talk doesn't have much to do with content. It is about how we say what we say and the attitude that comes across behind it. Gracious talk conveys that we like people. We are elevating speech to its highest purpose when we use it to benefit those around us.

The Bible encourages us to be gracious talkers in many ways. Proverbs 10:32 offers choice counsel along these lines: "The lips of the righteous know what is fitting." A "fitting" word is one that is the most helpful or appropriate at the moment. Proverbs 10:11 depicts the "mouth of the righteous" with an image of healing and restoring: it is "a fountain of life." Proverbs 16:24 compares "pleasant words" to a honeycomb because they both taste delicious and are nutritious, like a good breakfast cereal. They're good for us. Proverbs 25:11 asserts, "A word aptly spoken is like apples of gold in settings of silver"—a priceless treasure.

The right words at the right time are more valuable to us than anything. We treasure them always. We savor them, remembering them over and over again. We cling to a minister's carefully chosen words of comfort and hope at a funeral. A counselor's knowing words can restore our faltering marriage. The words to a special song come back to us when we need encouragement. Stirring speeches like those of Martin Luther King Jr., John F. Kennedy, Winston Churchill and Abraham Lincoln embed themselves in our cultural memory. In just this sense, words are eternal: people treasure them into eternity.

We don't want to just receive such priceless words of grace; we want to give them. We want some of our words to be so well chosen that someone carries them into eternity with them. We want as many of our words as possible to hit the spot.

Moses stands out as the most prominent gracious speaker in the Old Testament. His lack of confidence early on (Ex 4:10-17) is overshadowed by his growing astuteness in offering the best words for each moment, whether it is a moment of crisis or of celebration. The opening lines of his final speech to the children of Israel in Deuteronomy 32:2 serve as a fitting epitaph on his life and value of his words:

Let my teaching fall like rain
> and my words descend like dew,
like showers on new grass,
> like abundant rain on tender plants.

Joseph also catches our attention as one who speaks with grace. We encounter him first in Genesis 37 as a bragging teenager, but we watch him grow into a man who says no to adultery (Gen 39), brightens the lives of the cupbearer, the baker and even Pharaoh with good counsel (Gen 40—41) and dramatically forgives his brothers (Gen 42—47).

Others of note include Daniel, described in Daniel 1:4 as "well informed" and "quick to understand," who counsels the king but also speaks up for God in the face of enormous pressure. Esther's critical request to King Xerxes, "Spare my people," at just the right moment marks her as the epitome of gracious speakers (Esther 7:3). We could also note Samuel and any number of the prophets.

Encouragement to talk graciously does not end with the Old Testament. In the New Testament, Colossians 4:6 tells us, "Let your conversation be always full of grace." The passage has in view establishing good relationships with non-Christians through our gracious talk. Just before, verse 5 mentions "outsiders," calling us to be "wise" in how we deal with them. No doubt the intention is preevangelistic. Gracious talk is a way of attracting people to us so that they might hear the ultimate words of grace. We are encouraged to "make the most of every opportunity," to season our conversation "with salt" and "to answer everyone."

First Peter 3:15 makes a similar point, asking us to be prepared to respond with good answers to the real questions people have about Christianity. It, too, notes that we are to do this "with gentleness and respect," no matter how others might treat us. "Gentleness" is not the same Greek word as "grace," but it does convey similar ideas of being courteous and considerate of others. Second Timothy 2:25 uses it when it warns Timothy to instruct "gently" so as to give foolish, argumentative Christians a chance to come to their senses and repent. Philippians 4:5 uses the same word when it says, "Let your gentleness be evident to all," and Titus 3:2 joins it with being peaceable and humble "toward all."

Ephesians 4:29 attributes to gracious speech the awesome power of communicating God's grace: "Do not let any unwholesome talk come out of your mouths, but only what is helpful for building others up according to their needs, that it may benefit those who listen." The NIV translation here does a great job of conveying the idea of gracious speech, but it loses track of the special, Christian sense of "grace" that is intended in the second half of the verse. The last phrase should be translated "that it may impart *grace* to those who listen." This goes beyond just speaking words that make others feel good. Our words can carry the awesome grace of God.

Notice how verse 32 further connects this gracious speech to God's grace, saying, "Be kind and compassionate to one another, forgiving each other, just as in Christ God forgave you." Ephesians 5:1 goes on to imply that speaking graciously is part of imitating the attitudes and actions of God himself.

This is not easy for us to do. Our natural tendency is not to reflect God's image but to refract it, using our talk in sinful, harmful ways that do not lift people up but rather kick them down. We succumb to the speech sins described in chapters two and three of this book, even with people we love dearly.

Much of what we say is not blatantly sinful, though. We simply block real communication by thoughtless replies. A June 22, 1993, *USA Today* article surveys the content of Suzette Haden Elgin's book *Genderspeak,* which pinpoints language gender gaps. Elgin observes that certain common replies prevent people from engaging in meaningful communication. Some of these are all too familiar. Unsolicited advice starts off, "Let me tell you what I'd do." Diagnosis says, "You're only saying that because you're tired." Interrogations begin by demanding, "Why did you do that?" Contradictions assert, "You're not tired; you couldn't be." Hijackings declare, "You think you had a bad day? Let me tell you what happened to me!" Reassuring squelches philosophize: "A year from now you'll look back on this and laugh." "Cutesipation" soothes: "Of course I think your little stories are worth reading; they're charming." And of course, sermons moralize: "The money you spend on suits would clothe an orphanage."

The problem with all these kinds of responses is that wrong attitudes lurk below the surface of the words: superiority, arrogance, self-centeredness, coldness. Where is the warmth, the caring that seeks to understand what the other person is saying, that genuinely sympathizes with their problem, that desires to help? The words themselves are not the problem.

It is the attitude. Where is the grace of God?

Amazingly, it doesn't take many words to convey the grace of God in our conversations. The "pure religion" of James 1:27, which urges us to "look after orphans and widows," assumes that we will also give them kind words of encouragement and hope. Sirach 18:15 fills out the thought when it urges that rather than adding a reproachful word with a charitable gift, we should add a kind word, because "like dew that abates a burning wind, so does a word improve a gift." Verse 16 poignantly adds, "Sometimes the word means more than the gift."

A few kind words—"It'll get better," "How can I help?" "God loves you"—can go a long way toward communicating God's grace. But it's not always words alone; a friendly grin, a warm handshake, a pat on the shoulder can do it. Such gestures are also "gracious speech," because they come out of a gracious attitude that wants to convey that we care.

Learning to Speak with Grace

Suppose we want to do better. Suppose we want to turn our conversation around and make it more gracious. What do we do? Do we take a speech course at the local junior college, or a course in etiquette, or do we read the dictionary?

First, our plan is flawed if we assume that it's a simple matter of changing our words. Actors can put on words and take them off like wardrobe. They can drawl like Texans, enunciate like Bostonians or imitate "Valley girl" talk. Such talk isn't real. It is merely dramatic. Real words do not stand alone in a conversation. They come out of us. Our words are the end result of an intricate, mysterious, delicate process that takes place somewhere inside us.

Proverbs says this place is our heart: "If your heart is wise, . . . your lips speak what is right" (23:15-16). Proverbs 16:23 declares, "A wise man's heart guides his mouth." In Greek literature, this place is the mind. Philo observes that "the fountain of words" is the mind, the thoughts supplying substance and speech clarity.[1] Proverbs too can refer to thoughts, as in 21:29, "An upright man gives thought to his ways," or 14:8, "The wisdom of the prudent is to give thought to their ways."

The key New Testament passage in this regard is Matthew 12:34. Following the charge from the Pharisees that Jesus' power comes from Beelzebub, Jesus introduces the idea of blaspheming the Holy Spirit. He hints that this accusation his opponents are making isn't just about him. It is an affront against the Spirit of God, the One who provides him the power to cast out demons and do miracles. Then Jesus provides the rationale for basing irreversible judgment on one statement: "For out of the overflow of the heart the mouth speaks." Our heart anchors our words. So our words are fair game for judgment, as Jesus goes on to say in 12:37.

Whether we talk about the heart, the mind or the thoughts doesn't matter. We all know that our words come out of who we really are. This is tied up with our emotions, intellect, environment, education, self-worth, genetics and even diet. Anyway, gracious speech comes only from a gracious person with a gracious heart and mind.

Moses utters gracious speech through Aaron, his God-ordained mouthpiece (Ex 4:10-17). It doesn't matter that Moses is thick-tongued. It is his heart that is right. Despite Aaron's fluency with words, Aaron is not the man for the job. Samson may tell clever riddles (Judg 14:14, 18; 15:16), but he can hardly be described as having a gracious heart. On the other hand, Elihu, the mysterious fourth speaker in Job, offers God's words of grace with firm confidence because, as he says, "my words come from an upright heart" (Job 33:3).

Improving the graciousness of our speech, then, demands improving the graciousness of ourselves, or our hearts. But how do we make our hearts gracious?

The answer lies in our relationship with God. How much of ourselves are we willing to give over to God? How much will we open up to his influence? Elihu, in Job 33:4, says, "The Spirit of God has made me; the breath of the Almighty gives me life." Elihu speaks the gracious words of God because he lets God work though him. That's what you and I must do too.

We must open up our hearts and minds to God, for it is here that God is able to influence us. Philo astutely observes, "For without the prompter speech will give forth no utterance, and the mind is the prompter of speech, as God is of the mind."[2] We must make our minds and hearts fit places from which God can direct our thoughts and our talk. Philo says we must put our "faith in the God-sent love of wisdom"; this will help us speak "not only with ordinary gentleness but shout with a louder cry."[3] God, he says, will "whisper" good decisions to good people.[4]

But where is this wisdom from God? The rabbis point to Scripture: "He who gives his heart over to words of Torah is relieved of words of folly."[5] If we do this, our mouth, normally under our own control, can be "overpowered" by God for his use.[6]

So we begin with Scripture. Because Scripture is the Word of God, as we read it, listen to it, study it, we transfuse God's ways and values into our hearts. Over a lifetime of regular study, thinking God's thoughts and talking with grace become second nature to us. We find it easy to hear God's whisper. Our hearts overflow with gracious words.

Paul's words to Timothy in 2 Timothy 3:15-17 need to penetrate us. Paul sees value in the fact that Timothy has known Scripture "from infancy." Not only does it make him "wise for salvation," but it also makes him "thoroughly equipped for every good work." Scripture teaches, rebukes, corrects and trains us in righteousness because it is "God-breathed."

Like David in Psalm 25:4, we need to implore, "Show me your ways, O LORD," and then study his ways in Scripture for all we are worth. There is no substitute for listening to Scripture in our effort to transform our hearts into chambers of grace.

Our study of Scripture must go well beyond legalistic daily devotions or rote memorization. We must think hard about what the verses mean in their original context and how that translates into the contemporary context and our personal context. We must read good commentaries, interact with our pastors about their sermons, discuss the lessons with our teachers. This kind of study will make God the instructor of our hearts.

Still, an important warning bell should be sounded. No matter how much effort we put out to understand a passage of Scripture, a very real limitation remains. We cannot cross over the gulf between our human mind and God's wisdom by our own effort alone. We depend on God for that help, and he provides it in the person of the Holy Spirit.

In John 14:18 Jesus promises to his disciples that though he is going away, "I will not leave you as orphans." He has not caused us to be reborn into the world only to leave us alone and helpless now. As he goes to God, he sends us Another who lives in us and helps us know God and obey him. The Holy Spirit teaches us "all things" (v. 26).

Ephesians 1:13 asserts that every Christian has been marked with this "seal" of the Holy Spirit. Paul goes on in 1:17 to say that he prays fervently for God to give each one in the church "the Spirit of wisdom and revelation" for the express purpose that they might "know him better." This, he assumes, will open "the eyes of your heart" (v. 18). In 4:30, Paul shows that the presence of the Holy Spirit in our hearts is supposed to make a difference in our talk. He pleads with us not to talk ungraciously: "Do not grieve the Holy Spirit of God, with whom you were sealed for the day of redemption."

So the Holy Spirit bridges the gap between Scripture and our hearts. As he dwells within us, he helps us hear and understand Scripture. He latches onto meaning and gathers it into the storehouse of who we are. He slowly cures it within us so that its taste and smell subtly saturate our very being and it becomes one with us. As we grow, the Word of God grows with us. Our hearts grow in graciousness, and so then does our talk.

First Corinthians 2:13 expresses this truth about our speech well: "This is what we speak, not in words taught us by human wisdom but in words taught by the Spirit, expressing spiritual truths in spiritual words."

Can our talk become a vehicle of God's grace to the people you and I encounter each day? Can we get better at expressing God's love for every person by the way we talk to acquaintances, family members and friends? Indeed we can! Get to know God better by studying his Word. Be open to the Spirit within to help you understand and grow. Draw from these resources within for your speech. Through this, God will bless those around you beyond anything you will fully understand.

The Difficulty of Truthful Talk

Each of us can list many things that we find difficult to do. For you, the list might include hitting a golf ball, getting places on time or algebra. My list might include bowling a strike, keeping my office organized and reading a map. We see athletes on television do all kinds of things that seem incredibly difficult: marathon runners, weightlifters, Tour de France cyclists, quarterbacks, pitchers, race-car drivers, slam dunkers.

Despite variances among us about what we find difficult to do, I contend that one thing is hardest for all of us: telling the truth.

You can probably remember, as I do, times when a parent or teacher hovered over you, repeatedly insisting, "Tell the truth!" You fidgeted. You sweated. You closed your eyes. You bit your tongue. You did everything possible to keep the truth inside. Finally perhaps you mumbled, "Yes, I did it." Told to say it louder, you struggled against the truth again, but managed to say it distinctly. Asked if you were sure, if you really meant it, you may have screamed it out, and then cried and cried in your parent's arms.

Our struggle with truth and falsehood does not end with childhood. As adults, we still tend to suppress the honest truth until we are cornered. Half-truths, lies, deceptions continue to invade our speech despite our growing distaste for them.

One of the big problems with dishonesty is how it spoils life. Like a rotten potato, it spreads to affect everyone. I've seen a boy in a backyard baseball game swear he caught the ball on the fly, when everyone saw it bounce. I've watched a girl carefully manipulate the dice or the spinner in a board game to allow her to advance just the right amount of spaces and deny it to everyone. Such resistance to truth taints the whole game. It's ruined. The fun is spoiled for everyone.

Games mirror real life. Our continued resistance to truth as adults is evident in every arena of life. Politicians and lawyers are so infamous in this regard that we don't expect truth to come from their mouths. We don't expect truth from a car dealer, a salesman, a journalist, a doctor, even a judge or a minister. Truth cannot be found where we work, in our neighborhoods or even in our churches.

This vacuum of truth in our world burdens each of us. It invites us not to play by the rules anymore. It leads to rampaging violence in our streets and cities. Before our very eyes the quality of our lives spirals downward. Proverbs 19:22 says it is "better to be poor than a liar," because an honest poor person does more to benefit society than any kind of liar, who rips away at its very fabric. Sirach 20:24-26 even says, "It is better to be a thief than a habitual liar," since a thief's damage to society is on its exterior whereas a liar's is in its interior.

An October 9, 1992, *Time* article titled "Lies, Lies, Lies" nails all this on the head: "Lies flourish in social uncertainty, when people no longer understand or agree on the rules governing their behavior toward one another. During such periods, skepticism also increases; there will be a perception that more people are lying whether or not they actually are. That seems to be what is happening now."

The substance of the article certifies the public's perception and the reality of that perception concerning the 1992 presidential candidates George Bush, Bill Clinton and Ross Perot. A majority of Americans regarded as lies Bush's "no new taxes" pledge in 1988 and his "I was out of the loop" statement regarding the Iran-Contra debacle. A majority not only didn't believe but scoffed at Clinton's claim that he never inhaled marijuana. The article provides evidence to support these perceptions as well as evidence against Perot's statement that he cut short his navy career because his commanding officer wanted him to break rules.

Small wonder a poll cited in the article shows that 75 percent of Americans think less honesty exists in government than ten years previous, given their belief that the three major candidates for president in 1992 had lied, both in trivial matters and in critical ones.

Lying is so rampant among politicians that a not-so-tongue-in-cheek side-panel article appeared in the same issue of *Time* titled "Voters' Guide: How to Tell When a Politician Is Lying." It suggests suspicion when any politician cites statistics—the more precise the numbers, the more suspicion is called for. It warns us to be dubious about denials—the more specific the denial, the more likely that the person is hiding something in what was not denied. And a politician beginning with "Let me speak frankly . . ." is never telling the truth.

Avoidance of truth among politicians and government officials is just the tip of the iceberg. The tip is bad enough, but what lies below is just as bad and worse. Our society reeks for want of the truth. What can any of us do about this sad state of affairs?

The chances of reversing the cycle, of putting truth into play instead of falsehood, are not good.

First, in any situation the truth is outnumbered a zillion to one. An infinite number of ways exist to do anything but tell the truth or even discover the truth. The truth is at the center, surrounded by hordes of lies and shades of untruth. Rarely do we dare or are we able to hit dead center. It's easier not to. What is the truth in the Rodney King affair, the Tonya Harding incident, or even Watergate for that matter?

Second, there are many reasons to lie.[7] Usually we lie to protect ourselves. Wanting people to think well of us, we use lies as camouflage. Carefully we arrange them around us to hide our real self, who has done something wrong that we want no one to see. The fear of being discovered, our guilt exposed for all to see, fortifies our lies. Most criminal defendants swear their innocence no matter how good the evidence against them. They almost never confess on the witness stand as *Matlock* or *Perry Mason* portrays. We never outgrow the childhood denial syndrome, even with cookie crumbs on our face.

We also lie to get something we want: a job, a favorable income-tax return, a high grade, money. Often we think we deserve something even though we can't earn it fairly. Tonya Harding wanted a medal and to skate in the Olympics, so she denied involvement in injuring Nancy Kerrigan until after the games. Ivan Boesky and others lied about insider trading in order to get rich. My son will tell me he has cleaned his room to get his one-dollar allowance even though piles of belongings teeter on the edges of his desk.

We lie to impress people. We say we know things that we don't, we have done things that we haven't, or we are experts on things that we aren't. We will lie to impress a boyfriend, an employer, a teacher, even friends. What kind of friendships do we have when we think we need to impress our friends with lies about ourselves?

We intend lies like these to improve our relationships with others, but some lies we tell are conscious attempts to hurt people, maybe out of revenge or jealousy. Untruths carefully planted in the right ears can cut like knives. Proverbs 26:18-19 compares this kind of lying to "a madman shooting firebrands or deadly arrows," and Proverbs 15:4 says that deceit "crushes the spirit."

Sometimes, but rarely, we lie to help others. The concept of the noble lie is old. Long ago, despite arguing for high standards of truth in society, Plato argued that it is sometimes acceptable for physicians to lie to their patients and for rulers to lie to their subjects.[8] Yet such a notion is full of pitfalls.[9] The noble lie very quickly turns into abuse of power. In the Vietnam debacle, Watergate and Iran-Contra, many lies "in the interests of national security" were revealed to have been told in self-interest. The noble lie is also paternalistic and arrogant. Assuming we "know better," we rob people of their dignity and treat them like children. The noble lie is a cop-out. It avoids the more difficult but superior route of careful, sincere, gracious truth. Love demands the truth, not a lie.

This brings us to a third reason it is so difficult for us to tell the truth. Telling the truth sometimes inflicts pain. Telling the traumatic truth is so much harder than fabricating a noble lie. It's painful for a doctor to confront a patient with bad news, for a parent to inform a child that he or she wasn't chosen, for a friend to confront a friend with sin. Yet no one gains from shunning reality. Truth emerges out of loyalty, trust and respect, no matter how badly it may be received at first. Honest truth is always better than a well-meaning lie.

The Bible most often speaks to this issue in terms of reproof, which Proverbs 25:12 compares to "an earring of gold" and Psalm 141:5 likens to "oil on my head." The cold, hard truth is profitable and healthy for us. "A fool spurns his father's discipline," says Proverbs 15:5. Turning one's back to correction leads to "utter ruin," says Proverbs 5:12-14, but "whoever heeds correction gains understanding" (Prov 15:32). Proverbs 27:6 counsels, "Wounds from a friend can be trusted," and 24:26 exults, "An honest answer is like a kiss on the lips." Leviticus 19:17 commands, "Rebuke your neighbor frankly."

The New Testament views correction and reproof as essential components of a maturing Christian community.[10] Ephesians 5:21 tells us to "submit to one another out of reverence for Christ." Colossians 3:16

encourages us to "admonish one another with all wisdom." In Luke 17:3, Jesus says, "If your brother sins, rebuke him." What kind of "community" do we have if hard truths are never spoken, if confrontation is always avoided? It's superficial, fake, going through the motions, hollow.

Truth, then, struggles against many odds to get onto our lips. It's a wonder that truth emerges at all. But it does. Why? And what are the dynamics needed to help us talk truthfully?

Freeing the Truth

We value gifts. We treasure them. We can't wait to open them. Often the person giving us a gift is even more excited for us to open it than we are. Great care may have been taken to wrap it with bows and ribbons and lovely paper, to hide it away. It is hoped that the gift is something we can use, that we like, that will help us in some way. The best gifts are the ones that anticipate a need we didn't even know we had. When we get past the hubbub surrounding the gift, the wrapping, the "Happy birthday!" and the hugs and kisses, it is the gift itself that draws our attention. It is the gift itself that we will wear or set on the shelf or read or play with. It's the gift itself that will remind us of the happy moment when we received it.

Think of truth as a gift. Truth is the substance that provides value to our conversations. Communication, however it is trimmed, is worthless without truth. It's like an empty gift box sitting in the attic. The fact that it is branded with "Lord & Taylor" or "Neiman Marcus" doesn't matter. It's worthless, pointless, a crude joke. Imagine a conversation between two people who are lying to each other. Is anything of value happening there?

Without truth, talking is like muting the television. Contra the notions of Marshall McLuhan and other pundits, the medium is not the message. The message is the message. Truth is the value in talk that we walk away with, that improves our outlook on the world around us, that makes a difference in how we live and what we think. Truth is the basic ingredient of life. It's reality. Communication without truth is nothing.

Deep down we desire to hear the truth and tell the truth because truth grounds our existence. Despite rampant lying in business today, contracts, deliveries, prices and quality of products depend on a certain level of veracity for success and profit. We can look at government, home life and workplace in the same way: all require a minimal standard of truth, of reliability. But what I'm getting at here is much more fundamental than that.

None of us exist apart from the truth. According to Genesis, God has spoken the universe into existence. The truth of his word is the reality we live in. It is the substance of our being. Nowhere in this universe can we escape it.

So despite all the shackles we put on truth, it does and must emerge from our mouths. We can only temporarily and partially keep it chained.

The rabbis are right when they say truth sustains the world.[11] Yet Plato goes too far to assert that "truth stands first," even above the gods![12] Plutarch also misses the mark when he calls truth itself "a thing divine."[13] Truth is not an abstract principle hovering over the universe. No, it is embedded in the universe by the Creator. It emerges out of his personal character. He is the true God, who embodies all truth. As Deuteronomy 32:4 describes him,

He is the Rock, his works are perfect,

and all his ways are just.

A faithful God who does no wrong,

upright and just is he.

So when we lie, we deny "the Root" of our own existence, as some rabbis have said.[14] We betray God himself in a way the rabbis equate to idolatry.[15] Lying and falsehood are foreign elements in God's universe. To embrace them is to reject God.

No wonder we become so irate when our children or friends lie to us. It shakes us to the core because it shakes the universe to the core. Comedies make us laugh by following a character's lie with a clap of thunder or a flash of lightning. However, such images do reflect something of reality: every lie opens a crack in the seam of the universe. Lying wrongs God himself. Not only that, but when we lie we deal a setback to God's master plan to rid the world of falsehood.

Whether we like it or not, or even know it or not, each of us is part of a cosmic struggle between God and Satan which has everything to do with truth and falsehood. Satan, whom Jesus calls the father of all liars in John

8:44, uses our lies to enhance his effort to snatch God's universe away from him. When we lie we deny ourselves, and we undermine God. He needs us to let the truth out, not cover it over with selfish motives. He needs us to be true to the way he made us, true to the way he made the world.

In this great cosmic struggle, the truth of God is going to win out with or without our help. Satan will be cast into the Abyss (Rev 20:3). So we better get with the program.

The Qumran community, contemporary with early Christianity, was composed of conservative Jewish fanatics who fled from the corrupt practices of the temple into the desert. They had some far-fetched ideas, but in regard to truth and falsehood they are dead on. In the *Communal Rule*, their key document of incorporation, they prophesy (1QS 4:18-23),

> But in the mysteries of His understanding, and in His glorious wisdom, God has ordained an end for falsehood, and at the time of visitation, He will destroy it for ever. Then truth, which has wallowed in the ways of wickedness during the domination of falsehood until the appointed time of judgment, shall arise in the world forever. . . . There shall be no more lies, and all the works of falsehood shall be put to shame.

Proverbs 12:19 capsulizes this crucial thought in a simple way we can carry with us. "Truthful lips," it says, "endure forever, but a lying tongue lasts only a moment." From the perspective of eternity, that is exactly right. Truth is eternal, and when we speak the truth we step onto the threshold of eternity.

Letting the truth out has everything to do with character, being true to who we really are. Our ultimate model and source for this is God himself. He remains true to himself forever. It doesn't matter what Satan does to oppose him or what we do to disobey him. He never lies or shifts from the truth (Num 23:19). He never reneges on a promise, no matter how undeserving we are. When he speaks, it's "once for all," says Psalm 89:35. After a lifetime of personal, daily experience with God, Joshua lauds the integrity of God's character, saying, "Not one of all the good promises the LORD your God gave you has failed. Every promise has been fulfilled" (Josh 23:14).

Psalm 119:140 pictures God's speech as pure and uncontaminated, like gold that has been smelted and refined.[16] All his words "are true," says Psalm 119:160.

God knows that sin and evil pommel our lives and inhibit us from letting the truth out. He helps us in a number of ways.

First, he has planted the thirst for truth within each of us. Despite the difficulties we face in telling the truth, we feel good when it comes out. Holding it back makes us sick. Letting it out makes us feel whole. When we were children, our parents hugged us and we laughed after the truth came out. Something like that happens every time we tell the truth.

Also, when we discover the truth, whether it be a researcher finding a cure for cancer, a philosopher uncovering the meaning of knowledge, a housekeeper getting out a stain or a inquirer finding God in Jesus Christ, our reactions are like those in Jesus' parables of the lost coin, buried treasure and pearl of great price. We rejoice. We celebrate. We know we have found something invaluable when we have found the truth.

James 1:18 says that God "chose to give us birth through the word of truth," and James 1:21 implores, "Humbly accept the word planted in you." Primarily these passages focus on our new life in Christ and how the gospel makes it possible for us to be reborn and grow as children of God. However, the word *planted* usually means "innate," something one has from birth. For this reason, James may also have in mind what is expressed in Romans 1:18-25, that from birth every human has an inner knowledge of God that is repressed. The fact that we are all made in the image of God (Gen 1:26-27) becomes tangible not only in religious experience but also in our thirst for truth. God plants this lost piece of the puzzle to send us on our quest for him, but part and parcel of that is the search for truth.

Second, those of us who are Christians have an added bonus. Through Jesus Christ, we have already positioned the key puzzle piece in the right place. The ultimate mystery of the universe, the most important truth, has been discovered. Other pieces of the puzzle will connect much more easily in this perspective, just like finishing off a jigsaw puzzle. Truth becomes an even bigger priority for us and more accessible than before. That's what Colossians 3:9-10 means: Christ puts us on line so our new self can be "renewed in knowledge in the image of its Creator." Our transformation gives us a leg up on the evil within us that tries to keep truth muzzled.

Third, God helps us let truth out by providing a tangible model for us to follow. Yes, the Bible describes God's character and speech as true; but if God had not come to earth as a man in Jesus Christ, we could always point our finger at him and rightly say, "You don't know what we're up against down here!" But our excuse is gone. Jesus Christ has come. From embryo to birth to death, in Jesus God has experienced the excruciating difficulties we face in telling the truth. When Caiaphas point-blank asked Jesus if he was the Blessed One from God, he said yes. When God asked Jesus to die on the cross, take on the sins of humanity, the curse of God himself, Jesus didn't want to, but he said yes in the Garden of Gethsemane. He wrestled with the truth as you and I do. But the truth always came out. He remained true to who he was always. He proved that you and I can do it too.

Fourth, God helps us by providing the Holy Spirit. The same power Christ had with him to help overcome pressure against the truth has been given to us. Jesus says in that he gives us "the Spirit of truth" not just temporarily but "forever" (Jn 14:16-17), and he assures us that the Spirit will guide us "into all truth" (Jn 16:13). This includes the truth in Scripture, as pointed out earlier in this chapter. The Spirit also will help us discern the truth and tell the truth if we will let him fill us up and sweep away the barriers to truth within us. First Corinthians 2:15-16 says that we have "the mind of Christ," who helps us make "judgments about all things." We have every means Christ had to speak the truth, if we will use them.

Fifth, God helps us speak the truth by establishing the church. The church is founded on the most fundamental and important truth in the world, contained in the gospel of Jesus Christ. The gospel itself Paul calls "the word of truth,"[17] and the church's primary job is to safeguard this truth by honoring and preserving it in Scripture and in the preaching and teaching of Scripture. Christians are those who know the truth, are of the truth and are established in the truth, who live by it, walk in it and obey it.[18] The church aligns us with the truth from the outset. We live and breathe it daily. In the church we also have real-life models of integrity. We have leaders who are "above reproach" (1 Tim 3:2) in character, word and deed to encourage and guide us in speaking the truth.

Finally, in the church we have each other. We are mutually responsible for one another's growth and maturity in Christ (Eph 4:7-16), and that surely includes monitoring the integrity of each other's words as well as actions. We are supposed to confess our sins "to each other and pray for each other" (Jas 5:16). We are supposed to try to bring people back who "wander from the truth" (Jas 5:19). By "speaking the truth in love, we will in all things grow up into him who is the Head, that is, Christ" (Eph 4:15).

Throughout the ages, people have recognized that we can't get by without truth. Every culture, it seems, constructs ways of ensuring truth through various kinds of oaths. Although oaths work in many instances, they remain external and superficial means of enforcement. How many stacks of Bibles would it take to get some people to tell the truth, whether in court or anywhere else? People have always lied under oath, and they always will. The Old Testament and other ancient societies were as concerned about perjury as we are today. People will always lie, even under oath, if it serves their self-interest. The dire punishments facing many defendants in court make lying under oath all the more tempting. So what do we do?

Jesus says forget the oaths. Forget the external leverage. True speaking comes from within. It comes from a character that is being molded into the model of Christ through the power of the Holy Spirit.

Although others may not recognize the advantage Christians have in developing their character, many ancient writers perceived the problem with oaths. The Greek rhetorician Isocrates counsels, "Throughout all your life show that you value truth so highly that your word is more to be trusted than other men's oaths."[19] The Stoic Epictetus advises, "Refuse to take an oath at all, but if that is impossible, refuse as far as circumstances allow."[20] Cicero tells of a man whom the Athenians prevented from making court testimony under oath because "the Greeks did not wish it to be thought [that] the credibility of a man of proved honesty was more strictly secured by a ritual observance than by truthfulness of character."[21] "The lover of truth," says Aristotle, will be truthful "even when nothing depends on it."[22]

Jesus lays it on the line for us too. His utterance on this appears twice in Scripture, in Matthew 5:37 and in James 5:12.[23] The latter verse says, "Above all, my brothers, do not swear—not by heaven or by earth or by anything else. Let your 'Yes' be yes, and your 'No,' no, or you will be condemned." Honesty of character, talk that is true—these are essential trademarks of Jesus' followers. It's not that he's opposed to swearing an oath in court or in other social situations when convention calls for it. It's simply that he expects us to realize we are above all that. We don't need it. He provides all the motivation and all the resources we need to develop the kind of character that talks true, whether in court or anywhere else. We don't need to appeal to higher sources to back up our words, not even God himself. Our words are true, and everyone who ever interacts with us can count on it.

Combining Grace and Truth
This chapter has spent a lot of time establishing how vital both grace and truth are in our talk. Mostly we have concentrated on each separately. But we must be cautious. Nothing stated here should be taken to suggest that we can get along without one as long as we cultivate the other. Speaking the bald truth means something is missing. We haven't thought about or don't care to think about how best to express what we want to say. Speaking fluff is missing something too. It means we haven't put the time into having anything of substance to say. We should keep ourselves quiet until what we say combines grace and truth.

How do we know what that sounds like? Observe the life and ministry of Christ in the four Gospels. John 1:14 says that Jesus was "full of grace and truth." His Spirit can develop both in us at the same time too! Maybe we can't balance them perfectly as Jesus did. But we can do it, and we can do it better than we are doing now.

When grace and truth combine in our talk, the people around us will listen, and we will make a difference. God will speak through us to the hearts of others, and we will make the world a better place. Our words will resound in eternity.

Spiritual Communication

Talking to God

*M*ost of us, at some point in the day, pray. Some do it in the morning, some at night, others at random times during the day. Some pray a set prayer, others an extemporaneous one; some simply enter into quiet meditation. The orientation of one's prayer may be Islamic, Christian, Buddhist or maybe even nothing. People pray. We communicate to God and believe this to be the bedrock of our spiritual life.

Still, we are surprised by polls showing that 80 percent of Americans pray daily. We look around our place of work and don't see anyone praying. Rarely do we observe someone praying in a restaurant. Except for *The Simpsons,* television rarely shows people praying, nor do movies. Where is all this prayer happening?

The answer is that it is happening in people's private lives. People are praying when no one can watch. We pray when we are alone. We pray after the lights switch off at night. We pray in the early morning when no one else is up. We pray while the kids nap in the afternoon. We pray at lunchtime in the park. We pray while we jog, walk or work out. We pray while we drive. We pray for a fleet second at work—just a thought sent heavenward. Because it is private, we tend to keep quiet about it.

Second-century church leader Clement of Alexandria said simply, "Prayer is conversation with God."[1] But we should add that personal prayer is an incredibly private conversation. It's nobody else's business when, where, how or about what we pray. We don't need to know Jesus' injunction in Matthew 6:6 to pray "in secret" to realize that in prayer we talk to God alone. To seek privacy for this conversation seems natural. To keep to ourselves what happens in these most profoundly spiritual moments of our existence strikes us as right. To talk about our talks with God seems like breaking a trust with a dear friend. It seems wrong, sacrilege right up there with breaching the Holy of Holies. In Christian prayer, at least, we are our own priests communicating to God directly.

Certainly we do talk to God in groups. As congregations, as Bible study groups, as families, we pray together, joining our hands and our hearts. But even in these moments, although God certainly takes notice that a group is praying, he zeroes in on our private prayer within that group. Group prayer does not cancel out the reality that prayer remains personal, between me and God.

So we don't talk about our prayers much. We don't see each other pray much. All the while, though, we are praying up a storm.

This chapter assumes that just as talking to one another involves rights and wrongs, ethical principles surround our conversations with God. Awareness of appropriate and inappropriate ways of communicating with God will improve our maturing relationship with him. We will talk better. We will hear better. Our times alone with God will even be more meaningful than they already are.

Inappropriate Talk

One of the keys to good communication with God is realizing just whom we are talking to. This is not our pet schnauzer that we can command to sit in the corner or go get the paper. This is not our little brother whom we can order to get his toys out of our room or mind his own business. This is not our employer or coworker whom we can complain about behind her back. This is God, the Creator of the universe, the breath of our life, the knower of all things, the source of our being. Not to realize this from the beginning of our relationship can lead to costly mistakes when we try to talk to him.

We should never speak to God without the respect he is due simply for who he is. No matter what else we have to say, he deserves this.

I suppose our parents present the closest parallel. From our earliest days they provide protection, comfort, nourishment and discipline. We learn to depend on them and appreciate them. Occasional conflict with them may prompt disrespectful words, but these are words we later regret. Even as we grow into adults and the relationship with our parents becomes more mutual, we know that respect should underlie our every conversation with them. Because they are sinners, sometimes they do or say things that make them unworthy of respect. But we talk to them respectfully simply because they are our father and mother. Nothing is ever going to change that.

Our basic relationship with God doesn't change either. Just as he gave birth to the nation of Israel and called them his children, so also he gives birth to us through Jesus Christ and calls us his children. True, he wants us to grow up into maturity. He wants us to nurture a mutual relationship with him like the one Abraham had, so close that he could be called "God's friend" (Jas 2:23; see also 2 Chron 20:7; Is 41:8). God doesn't want us to continue to be like babies forever. He wants us to be good friends. However, our adult friendship with him cannot ever lose sight of who it is we are talking to.

Moses failed to uphold God's holiness before the children of Israel when he struck the rock at Meribah-Kadesh, and for this God denied him entry into the Promised Land, his life's greatest ambition (Num 20:12; 27:14; Deut 32:51). So for us, no matter how close we become to God, certain words are forever out of bounds. Many of these run parallel to the "speech sins" discussed in chapters two and three.

In the Qumran community one was never to speak the name of God for any reason, not even when it occurred in a reading from Scripture. If one spoke his name or failed even accidentally to make a proper substitution for the four Hebrew letters (יהוה) that are pronounced "Yahweh," that person was immediately and permanently ousted from the community. God's personal name was deemed too holy to be on the sinful lips of human beings.

This goes too far and majors in minors. Speaking God's name certainly is not disrespectful in and of itself. However, in certain circumstances it could be. We could be presumptuous and overfamiliar. We could speak to him as if to a fishing buddy, disregarding the fact that his position is more like that of a forest ranger. We could call him "Daddy" without establishing a relationship as "Father."

Because I am a professor with a Ph.D., students usually call me "Professor Baker" or "Dr. Baker." For a freshman to call me "Bill" would presume a relationship that we don't have—it would be offensive. A graduate with whom I have formed a personal friendship over the years, however, is in a different category. She might continue to call me "Dr." out of habit, but she doesn't need to; at this point I would prefer to be called "Bill."

Moses attained a relationship with God that was personal, conversational, full of give-and-take. The Bible shows him talking one-on-one to God more than anyone else. Yet the ground rules were set at their first meeting. From within the burning bush God's very first words to Moses were "Do not come any closer. . . . Take off your sandals, for the place where you are standing is holy ground" (Ex 3:5).

So it is when we come to God to talk. The ground doesn't get less holy just because we get to know him better. If anything, we realize more and more how holy it is, how holy and wonderful he is, as we grow in our relationship with him.

Our pact with God involves not only respect when we approach him to talk but also awareness that speaking his name anytime is holy. This doesn't mean that we, like the members of Qumran, never utter his name. It does mean that we never speak his name lightly, without recognition and full awareness of whose name we have spoken.

The third commandment is "You shall not misuse the name of the LORD your God" (Ex 20:7)—or, as it is often translated, "You shall not take the name of the Lord your God in vain." Vanity is about using other things in the sole interest of making ourselves look good. The clothes, the hair mousse, the jewelry, the hours in front of the mirror, the Nautilus, the car—these things serve to promote our image. We can't use God's name like a decoration without defaming it. Certainly such misuse would include saying "God damn it!" to voice our anger. But it also includes the ever-popular expression "O-my-God!" which many seem to consider appropriate for just about any occasion these days.

While I'm at it, I may as well take a swipe at Christian trinkets, T-shirts and trivia. Somehow I can't help but wonder whether God isn't somehow defamed when I wear him to match my shorts, or when I stick him in my pocket to write with, no matter how true the message on the T-shirt or the pen.

To invoke God's name is serious business. Even when we are not talking to him, we must voice his name in a way that preserves and promotes his holiness. We should uphold his honor as we do that of our own family.

The Bible warns us of another, related way in which we might speak to God inappropriately. Making false vows and oaths also misappropriates God's name for personal gain and fails to honor God's holiness.

In the Old Testament a vow is usually a two-party agreement involving a person and God, in which the person pledges to give something to God in return for his favor or blessing. It may be an act of worship or commitment to God. Jacob vows to make Bethel a shrine and to give a tithe to God, if God will take care of him (Gen 28:20-22). Hannah vows that if God blesses her with a son, she will dedicate the child to him (1 Sam 1:11-28).

An oath seals a three-party transaction: God is called upon as a witness to the truthfulness of two people. One or both will swear before God that the agreement will be kept, giving God license to mete out just punishments if it isn't. David swears to Jonathan that Saul is trying to kill him (1 Sam 20:3). Ruth swears her allegiance to Naomi in Ruth 1:17, "May the LORD deal with me, be it ever so severely, if anything but death separates you and me." God himself swears on the integrity of his own character.

Despite the aversion to swearing in God's name that we see in Qumran and in New Testament times,[2] the people of Israel are told point-blank in Deuteronomy 6:13 to swear by his name only. To swear by anything other than God is an insult to his character. He alone is the moral fiber of this universe.

Using God's name in an agreement has its downside, though. One cannot break the agreement without reaping dire consequences. God's name will not be identified with a lie. Leviticus 19:12 warns, "Do not swear falsely by my name and so profane the name of your God. I am the LORD."

Similarly, the God whose own words and deeds are one, who never rescinds a pledge, does not overlook a pledge voluntarily committed to him. One must come to terms with the seriousness of pledging to God before undertaking it. As Numbers 30:2 says, the person who makes such a promise "must not break his word but must do everything he said." God is an exacting landlord and does not tolerate even a late payment, as Deuteronomy 23:21-22 spells out: "If you make a vow to the LORD your God, do not be slow to pay it, for the LORD your God will certainly demand it of you and you will be guilty of sin. But if you refrain from making a vow, you will not be guilty."

We are better off not to make a vow or oath than to make one and break it. Jephthah's reckless vow in Judges 11:30-31 cost his virgin daughter her heart's desire. Zedekiah's oath of loyalty to Nebuchadnezzar cost him his life (2 Chron 36:13; Jer 52:3; Ezek 17:11). Israel lost its lands and went into captivity because of the people's broken vows to God. And so you and I must heed the advice of Ecclesiastes 5:5-6, drawn from Deuteronomy 23:21-23: "It is better not to vow than to make a vow and not fulfill it. Do not let your mouth lead you into sin."

Sometimes we make deals with God when we are in a crisis. We attempt to barter our time, money or spirit for some kind of rescue or achievement. "Get me out of this mess, Lord, and I will go to church every Sunday." "Help me pass this exam, and I will read the Bible." "Heal my daughter, and I will give money to support the halfway house." Bargains like these are vows. We had better be careful with them and recognize their seriousness. We cannot buy God's action on our behalf, but when he comes through for us, we must come through for him or reap the consequences.

We cannot trifle with God's honor without repercussions. Whether we are parents dedicating our newborn child to God, a couple swearing before

God to cleave to each other forever or a sinner confessing a commitment to Jesus Christ as Lord, when we utter God's name we seal a commitment that we must honor.

Inappropriate talk to God can take an even more foolish and dangerous turn. In the discussion of slander back in chapter two, we saw that from a biblical perspective it is one of the most heinous speech crimes that one person can carry out against another—it is repeatedly compared with murder. Yet as vile as slander is against fellow men and women, it is nothing compared to the sin of slandering God, or blasphemy.

Our understanding of blasphemy usually focuses on a person's claim to be God; this is how the Jewish leaders charged Jesus. We are sure we'd never be so stupid as to claim to be God. We aren't egomaniacs like Nero or Hitler.

Yet the Bible generally views blasphemy more broadly as slandering God, not necessarily standing in God's place.[3] It is the shameless audacity of insulting his honor on purpose. It includes reviling God's character to others as well as shaking our fist at God and challenging him to strike us dead. It involves spreading false information about God in order to drive people away from him. The blasphemer knowingly speaks against God in a way that causes his name to be slandered.

The most notorious blasphemer in the Old Testament is Sennacherib, king of Assyria, who through his messenger disdainfully attacks God and his power to rescue his people, also mocking Hezekiah and the "foolishness" of those like him who trust in God.[4] Defending his honor, God protects Jerusalem and slays Sennacherib's 185,000-man army while they sleep. The Edomites also mark themselves as blasphemers for laughing at the fall of Jerusalem in Ezekiel 35:12, and God marks them for annihilation because of this.

We wouldn't think Israel could blaspheme God, given the Old Testament's ample record of the many times he came through for them. However, they blaspheme him on numerous occasions and in a variety of ways. They blaspheme God by casting scorn on his ability to deliver them into the Promised Land (Num 14:11, 23), by deriding his ability to provide them food and water in the desert (Num 20:10; Ps 78:18-19), by spitefully worshiping idols (Is 65:7; Ezek 20:27), by rejecting his laws and despising his words (Is 5:24), by speaking lies against him (Hos 7:13-14), by questioning his love for them and his knowledge of their circumstances (Ezek 9:9), by denying his ability to exercise justice (Ezek 33:17; Mal 2:17) and by arrogantly questioning the value of being his people (Mal 3:13-15).

It's easy to regard blasphemy as something someone else does. But when we contemplate this list of blasphemous actions by Israel, we realize that blasphemy can enter our own talk. Do we look at reports of starving children or slaughtered tribes and dismiss God's justice? Do we knowingly turn away from what is right in the eyes of God? In a crisis do we look to heaven despisingly and scream, "Why me, Lord?" When we speak to God scornfully, insulting and undercutting his credibility in the eyes of those around us, we are slandering God, blaspheming his name.

Does this mean we shouldn't be honest in expressing our true feelings toward God when we speak to him? Absolutely not! However, we can—and do at times—cross the line between honest expression and unacceptable contempt. When believers do such a thing, it can add fuel to the fire of those around us who already are skeptical toward God.

James 4:13-17 implies that simply ignoring God in our day-to-day life is blasphemy. It pictures a businessman planning an extended trip that he expects will make him a lot of money. James is critical of him because he takes care of every aspect of the trip except the most important: he forgets to seek God's will. He ignores his dependence on God for any kind of success. He acts as though he had complete control over his life. He plans as though he were the center of the universe.

James reminds him, and us, that in the expanse of God's eternal sovereignty we are like a morning mist that burns off by 8:00 a.m. God remains the Father whose permission and blessing we need for each day. Yet we find it all too easy to overvalue our importance and insult God in the process. James identifies arrogance and boasting as the root of this kind of blasphemy, as of all other kinds.

We see this in God's response to Sennacherib when he blasts,

Who is it you have insulted and blasphemed?
    Against whom have you raised your voice
and lifted your eyes in pride?
    Against the Holy One of Israel! (2 Kings 19:22)

As with all speech, it's not just words that are blasphemous; it is the attitude, the real feelings that words convey. Any kind of arrogance or pride in the presence of God is not only foolish boasting but blasphemy. In his haughtiness, the wicked man says, "There is no God" (Ps 10:4 NASB). Our response to encountering God, in contrast, ought to be like Isaiah's: "Woe to me! . . . I am ruined! For I am a man of unclean lips, and I live among a people of unclean lips" (Is 6:5).

Blasphemy is not limited to our attitude and response to God. Already in the Old Testament, we see that God is blasphemed by those who heap disparaging remarks upon *his people*. The New Testament expands this concept and applies it to the Christian community. James 2:7 charges wealthy non-Christians with "slandering the noble name of him to whom [Christians] belong." They are not doing this by cursing or slandering Christ directly. The previous verse explains that they are "exploiting" believers and "dragging [them] into court." They denigrate Christ by sullying the character of his followers.

James 3:9 takes this concept of indirect blasphemy of God even further by implying that anytime we curse a fellow human being we are, in fact, blaspheming God, because God made us all. With this principle, the entire discipline of talk ethics comes under the umbrella of honoring or dishonoring God in what we say. It is a daunting task that requires great care and lots of help.

Since Jesus Christ is divine, any disparagement of him is blasphemy, according to the New Testament. Blasphemy includes not only the cursing of Christ but also the denial of Christ, rejection of his message, turning away from him to follow false teaching, and unbecoming behavior by Christians.[5] Blaspheming the Holy Spirit by attributing Jesus' exorcising power to Beelzebub is even more serious, bearing eternal consequences (Mt 12:22-32; Mk 3:22-30; Lk 22:65; 23:39).

We probably can't imagine ourselves blaspheming Christ. That's what Peter thought too. Yet he denied Christ three times (Mk 14:66-72). True, he was under great pressure and feared for his life. But isn't "crunch time" when you and I also find it the most difficult to proclaim our allegiance to Christ? We live in a world that denies the validity of Christ with every breath.

This puts tremendous pressure on us to conform rather than stand up and speak out for Christ. When we succumb to this pressure, we blaspheme Christ.

We also blaspheme Christ whenever our behavior or talk bring his name into disrepute. Disrespect of our boss denigrates the name of Christ. So does lying or cheating or harming others.

Inappropriate talk toward God can take many forms; however, the bottom line for *appropriate* speech is remembering who he is and not forgetting who we are when we talk to him. Honor, not flippancy, and humility, not arrogance, are the attitudes we need each day as we grow in our relationship with God. Our model is the attitude of the tax collector who says, "God, have mercy on me, a sinner" (Lk 18:13). It's not that of the Pharisee who proclaims, "God, I thank you that I am not like other men" (Lk 18:11). The rule of thumb in relating to God—or to anyone, for that matter—is spelled out at the end of this parable: "For everyone who exalts himself will be humbled, and he who humbles himself will be exalted" (18:14).

Appropriate Talk

That we can talk to God is a mystery, one of the greatest mysteries of the universe we live in. How is it that in the flick of an instant we can be talking to God? One moment we are thinking to ourselves or talking to our husband and then—boom, just like that, we are ushered into God's throne room to say whatever it is we want to say. As St. Teresa of Ávila reflects, "We are always in the presence of God, yet it seems to me that those who pray are in his presence in a very different sense."[6] I can't explain that. I can't explain our personal communication line to the Creator. However, I can make some recommendations about how best to use this amazing aspect of life that God has provided us.

First, we are called to praise. Thousands of years ago, the devoutly Jewish people of Qumran, who dedicated every moment of their day to prayer, penned a thought in their hymnbook worth our pondering. They declared that God's very purpose in creating speech was so that we "may tell of your glory and recount your wonders" and that "your name may be praised by the mouth of all men."[7] If there is any truth in this—and I believe there is—then our voices attain their highest potential when we use them to praise God.

The Qumran people also believed that their liturgy was a replica of what the angels sing in heaven.[8] I won't go that far, but I do believe praise is an ongoing quality of heaven and that if we plan to be there, we may as well get plenty of practice now.

The most appropriate words we can say to God, then, express praise and adoration. Words of praise should emerge naturally from us in appreciation of who he is and how much he has done for us. They should roll off our tongue at the beginning of every talk with God. They should arise from our mind throughout the day. Psalm 100:4 says, "Enter his gates with thanksgiving and his courts with praise." Psalm 118:1 advises, "Give thanks to the LORD, for he is good; his love endures forever."

Though our mouths are designed for praising God, one of the frustrations of praising God is that we run out of words. Our words seem so trivial when compared to the One they are trying to describe and the bounty for which they attempt to give thanks. Who can utter the number of thank-yous that God deserves? Who can describe his greatness? The rabbis say God deserves "a thousand thousands and a million millions of benedictions" from each one of us.[9] In Sirach 42:15—43:35 the author attempts to enumerate all the great works of God but then concludes that they are inexhaustible and that humankind cannot fathom the whole of God. But rather than giving up on praising God because of this, he concludes that it should give us impetus to praise him all the more.

A wise rabbi, commenting on Psalm 88:1, attempts to reflect God's perspective on all this: "Praise Me in any way you desire to praise Me, and I will condone whatever your manner of praising Me, for no one can discover even one of the many kinds of praise which are appropriate for the Holy One."[10]

We don't fault a child for not knowing how to say anything more than "thank you" for something she appreciates. We treasure her words. We don't expect our children to run down an exhaustive list of everything we have done for them every time they speak to us. We do expect thanks, though, and we appreciate it each time we receive it, however inadequate it might be.

God is like this too. He enjoys our praise but understands our limitations.

The Old Testament describes a "firstfruits" offering in which Jews gave to God the first of the wool, grain and wine produced on their farms (Ex 23:16; 34:22; Deut 18:4). This is what praise is for us when we speak to God. It is the firstfruits of our lips. It is the first. It is the best of what we have to say to God. And he deserves our best effort to praise him. As Psalm 96:4 enjoins, "Great is the LORD and most worthy of praise."

Second, the Bible encourages us to sing our words to God. The call to praise God in song leaps from the pages of the Psalms.[11] Indeed, many of the psalms are intended to be sung. Moses sings. David sings. Solomon sings. And so does Mary, the mother of Jesus, and Zechariah, the father of John the Baptist.[12] Psalm 96:11 says that even the heavens and the earth sing to God.

Why should we sing? Primarily, singing arises from our joy in God's blessing. Psalm 95:1 says, "Come, let us sing for joy to the LORD; let us shout aloud to the Rock of our salvation." James 5:13 recommends, "Is anyone happy? Let him sing songs of praise."

Singing helps us release our emotions. It allows our deepest feelings to join forces with our profoundest words to make them say more than they do alone. Our words are enhanced. Our communication with God reaches another level when we sing it.

Singing is so natural, too. As adults, we seem to lose track of this and try to cover over our feelings. But just watch a child. If he is at all happy, it won't be long before we'll hear him singing, borrowing a line or two from something he has heard, adding whatever comes to mind. Singing is an integral part of a child's happiness and joy.

As adults who desire to tell God our truest thoughts and feelings, we need to release that child in us who loves to sing. Make up your own tunes and sing your prayers to God sometimes. Sing along with a praise tape in the car. Shock the people in your pew at church and sing the hymns and choruses lustily for a change—as the song leader says, "like you really mean it."

When you sing, you will find yourself saying things, revealing things to God, that wouldn't come out otherwise. Your guard will slip down. Your real thoughts and feelings will flood out. And God will be pleased. He will revel in your deep and honest communication. He will hear and respond. Whether in church or in the privacy of your personal prayer life, "sing and make music in your heart to the Lord," as Ephesians 5:19 urges, and new riches of communication with God will unfold for you.

Third, confession is appropriate in our communication with God. Acute awareness of our sinfulness can't be avoided when we come into the presence of our perfect, loving Creator. Despite our growing relationship with him, we never get past the vast gulf between us and him. In him is goodness and love. In us is evil and hate. We look as in a mirror at every ideal and potential God has for us and see the horror of our sinfulness in contrast. Guilt overwhelms us.

"Grieve, mourn and wail," invites James 4:9, because true expression of guilt involves our emotions. To impassively recite, "God, forgive me all my sins," every night does not cut it. Realization of our sin should cut us to the quick. Sometimes it will reduce us to tears and sobs, as when our parents confronted us with wrong when we were children. Our sin should upset us, and we should show it in our prayers to God.

We can't hide our sin from God anyway. As Proverbs 5:21 says, "For a man's ways are in full view of the LORD, and he examines all his paths." So we may as well be upfront about them. God will respond with compassion and forgiveness. Proverbs 28:13 declares, "He who conceals his sins does not prosper, but whoever confesses and renounces them finds mercy."

Guilt will eat us alive, but God's forgiveness will wash us clean and restore us. David expresses this truth vividly in Psalm 32:3-5:

When I kept silent,
> my bones wasted away
> through my groaning all day long.

For day and night
> your hand was heavy upon me;

my strength was sapped
> as in the heat of summer.

    Then I acknowledged my sin to you
        and did not cover up my iniquity.
    I said, "I will confess
        my transgressions to the LORD"—
    and you forgave
        the guilt of my sin.

Of course we can't spend all our prayer time listing our sins; the list is inexhaustible, and we are not fully conscious of all of them anyway. Still, we can and must face squarely the ugly side of ourselves routinely, or else the rest of our talk with God rings hollow and our so-called relationship with God is a façade.

Fourth, it is appropriate for us to bring requests to God. Our requests acknowledge our dependence as well as his magnitude. Psalm 105:4 admonishes us, "Look to the LORD and his strength." Psalm 34:8 invites, "Taste and see that the LORD is good; blessed is the man who takes refuge in him."

It is God's nature to give and to bless. He wants us to reach our fullest potential. He wants us to enjoy the life he has given us. He wants us to see that he alone is the One who truly satisfies. When we ask and he fulfills, there can be no doubt in our minds that he is there and is lovingly watching over us.

James 1:17 proclaims that "every good and perfect gift is from above," and James 1:5 insists that God "gives generously to all without finding fault." Whether we ask or not, God blesses our lives. But when we do ask, God blesses us even more. God does not want to withhold his bounty. He wants to share it with us. And we should never be afraid to ask. Unlike our boss or some of our friends, God will never, ever look down on us for voicing our heart's desire. On the contrary, he will be pleased that we have asked, even if he can't give it to us.

Around my house I am Mr. Fix-it. My children and my wife regularly bring me things to fix. Whether it is a toy or an appliance, I get a crack at it before it gets tossed or taken to a repair shop. Although I am concerned and irritated sometimes about how something got broken, I want my wife and children to be happy, and I will fix it if I can. Even if I can't fix it, it makes me feel good that they have come to me believing that I can.

I believe God responds to us like this. He likes it when we come to him for help. He loves us and will do what he can. Whatever his response, it will be in our best interests. Jesus says it this way in Matthew 7:9-11: "Which of you, if his son asks for bread, will give him a stone? Or if he asks for a fish, will give him a snake? If you, then, though you are evil, know how to give good gifts to your children, how much more will your Father in heaven give good gifts to those who ask him!"

It is essential for us to recognize, though, that God cannot fulfill our every request. At Gethsemane Jesus pleads that the cup of death and punishment for our sins pass by him. This expresses his genuine desire. Yet he knows and acknowledges that God's plans stretch beyond him as an individual, even as God's incarnate Son. "Not as I will, but as you will," he stresses in Matthew 26:39. His own prayer corresponds to the way he teaches us to pray: "Your kingdom come, your will be done" (Mt 6:10).

God has the power to grant our requests, but he also has the insight to know when he shouldn't. Not only does he have an overarching plan for the redemption of humanity and the universe in process, but he also has the best interests of every individual in his mind. What if your request would set back someone's salvation? What if a sunny day for you would mean lost crops for farmers?

So of course God will not fulfill our every request, and we can gladly acknowledge, even if we don't always say so, that he knows best and will do what he can to meet our needs but that he has other things to consider. Our goal, really, in our relationship with him, is increasingly to improve our desires to match his will.

Our requests to God should not just be about ourselves, either. Our prayers should reflect our knowledge and concerns about the needs of others. Examples of such prayer are numerous in the New Testament. Jesus prayed for his disciples (Jn 17:9-16). Paul prayed for the people in the churches.[13] The church in Jerusalem prayed for the church in Corinth (2 Cor 9:14).

Of course we find it easy to pray for our friends and family. But we should consider no one outside our domain of prayer. First Timothy 2:1 says that "requests, prayers, intercession and thanksgiving [should] be made for everyone." Verse 2 specifically names "kings" as people whom early Christians had a hard time praying for. In Matthew 5:44 Jesus says, "Pray for those who persecute you."

In this day of political activism among many evangelical Christians, many of us find it all too easy to get caught up in the cutting rhetoric of Rush Limbaugh and other liberal-bashers. But are we praying for leaders whose policies we disagree with?

It's easy to complain about the person at work who gives us a hard time, but are we praying for her? Are we as concerned for her spiritual welfare and God's place in her life as we are for our self-justification? Can we envision our strife with someone else as within the realm of God and pray about it? We need to talk about these things in our prayers.

Fifth, not just appropriate but absolutely essential to our talks with God is honesty—total, sincere, abject honesty. This book has already discussed how essential honesty is in the ethics of talking with people. That goes double or triple for talking to God. For one thing, God knows all about us anyway. We can hide nothing, absolutely nothing. It's as foolishly schizophrenic as trying to hide something from ourselves. In fact, he knows us better than we know ourselves.

In Psalm 17:1-3 David speaks of how God probes his heart, examining his motives and integrity. He assures God that his prayer is sincere and honest, that "it does not rise from deceitful lips." He knows that this is essential in order for God to "give ear to [his] prayer." God's attention and response are directly proportional to David's truthfulness. In Psalm 145:18 David states this as a principle for us all: "The LORD is near to all who call on him, to all who call on him in truth."

Our prayers cannot be self-indulgent Christmas lists. God sees through this kind of worldliness in a second and turns stone-cold to us. Why would he give us things that are just going to draw us further away from him? James 4:3 plainly answers our spoiled-brat cry of "Unfair!" when it says, "When you ask, you do not receive, because you ask with wrong motives, that you may spend what you get on your pleasures."

Not only will wrong motives derail successful communication with God, but so will lack of conviction. We "must believe and not doubt," James 1:6

encourages us, "because he who doubts is like a wave of the sea, blown and tossed by the wind." Lack of conviction in our prayers points to a lack of faith in God generally. Such a person is "double-minded," or more literally "double-souled." Spiritually, he is a sea of confusion, trusting in God one day but scorning him the next. Perhaps at youth group he is influenced by his Christian friends; at school he follows his non-Christian friends. He doesn't really know what he believes about God for himself. "That man," says James 1:7, "should not think he will receive anything from the Lord."

James's teaching reflects what we also see in Matthew 21:22 and Mark 11:22-24. Asking "in faith" is part and parcel with asking "in truth." Confidence in God, in his wisdom, his love, his power, should encourage us to speak from our heart, knowing that he will hear and act in kind. This does not mean that we will get everything we ask for. It does mean that real, personal communication with God takes place, and he will act on our behalf.

Some leaders in our day present themselves to the Christian public as having a special inside track to God. They cultivate loyal followers who send in prayer needs, which they voice on television or radio. The Bible, however, rejects the idea that powerfully effective prayer is the domain of just a handful of Christians. James 5:17 emphasizes that "Elijah was a man just like us." Elijah's prayers were so powerful they could begin and end a three-and-a-half-year drought, yet the "righteous" life of an Elijah can be cultivated by each of us. Elijah's earnestness and conviction in prayer are possible for all of us.

That is the wonder of it all. God will hear, and he will act in response to your prayers and mine without favoritism, without bias. All he asks is that we talk to him in truthfulness and faith.

This pertains even to those dark truths within ourselves we don't think he would want to hear. I recall so vividly what the popular Roman Catholic writer John Powell said once when speaking to a group of college students. Sometimes, he said, he gets up in the morning and cries out, "O God, I don't want to be priest today! I'm tired, drained from counseling, from teaching, from serving the needs of people." Is God horrified by such candor? Does he turn away? Of course not! It is the honest truth. God will minister to the despair, the weariness. He will lift his servant up to be all that he can be on that day. And so after praying such a prayer, Powell says, he rises filled with God's power to be a priest that day.

The Jewish rabbis coined one word to include all that is required for successful prayer. The word is *kawwanah.* It encompasses all that we have been talking about: honesty, sincerity, pure motives, submission. The rabbis said it doesn't matter where a person is or what he is doing. He could be in corporate worship reciting a liturgical prayer or plowing in his field offering up a spontaneous thought. If he has *kawwanah,* God hears his prayer. It is *kawwanah* that we have been talking about.

Sometimes we think wrongly that we need to be in a special place at a special time to speak with God. Of course it's good to have a prayer routine. But we rob ourselves of some of the best opportunities for good communication with God when we put him on a schedule. God needs to become so intertwined with our life that we are constantly lifting thoughts to him. Christian singer Cliff Richard calls such prayer "spontaneous mental chat."[14] God is ready and waiting patiently at all times to talk to us. We just need to lift up our hearts and speak honestly to him at any time—at all times.

God waits patiently, encouraging us, prodding us to realize and to utter our honest feelings and thoughts to him. It's like charades. God is like the person trying to get her team to guess the movie title. She knows they know what it is, if she can get them to piece it together. Just as she is gleeful when someone recognizes one of her clues, God is delighted when he has helped us utter some buried truth about ourselves. Whether it is a sorrow or a pain, a sin, a joy, a need, a hope or a fear, spiritual progress is made when we discover and express it to our waiting Father.

Finally, we should pray in the name of Christ through the power of the Holy Spirit. In John 14:14 and 16:24, Jesus is very specific with his disciples: from now on, he explains, they should pray "in my name." This truth stands as a pillar of Christian faith and practice. Having obediently suffered death for the sins of human beings, Christ now stands as the eternal mediator between God and humankind (1 Tim 2:5). Hebrews 7:25 asserts, "He always lives to intercede for them."

It's all too easy for us to make this vital reality a mere formality in our prayers. We end our prayers with the words "in Jesus' name" without a thought of their significance. Our prayers ought to contemplate what Christ means to us and express joy and thanksgiving for the great sacrifice Christ made on our behalf. Jesus volunteered for God's rescue mission to save us, and we should never forget it. When we talk to God, focus on Jesus should be regular and thoughtful.

Jesus is completely aware of our shortcomings. He knows the difficulty we face in communicating with God, even if we have *kawwanah*. Our heart's desire seems so trivial sometimes, so selfish. Like Job, we find that before God our words get stuck in our throat. They seem inadequate.

An essential part of Christ's intercession for us addresses this problem. He gives us the Holy Spirit, really his spirit—"Christ in us." One of the many purposes of the Spirit in us is to help us pray. Not only does the Spirit lead us in gracious and truthful talk with one another, as we discovered in chapter six, but he also helps us in the same way with the Father. Romans 8:26 teaches, "In the same way, the Spirit helps us in our weakness. We do not know what we ought to pray for, but the Spirit himself intercedes for us with groans that words cannot express."

The Spirit knows us and he knows God. His job is to fashion our unique being in accordance with the will of God. Increasingly, he helps our will and God's will to unify. As he does this with our life, he does this also in our talks with God. He "intercedes for the saints in accordance with God's will," says Romans 8:27. He helps our *kawwanah* reach beyond words to spiritual communication with God.

Ephesians 6:18 tells us to "pray in the Spirit on all occasions with all kinds of prayers and requests." This is not an option for meaningful, spiritual communication with God. It is necessary. But how does it happen? What is the difference between praying in the Spirit and not doing so?

Some Christians may contend that this verse calls us to some kind of special prayer language or speaking in tongues. I hesitate to agree, since speaking in tongues is not a gift the Spirit gives to all, and his action here works in all believers, even though it may not happen every time we pray.

Neither does the verse advocate some kind of Eastern meditation in which we lose consciousness. Ephesians 6:18 connects praying in the Spirit to a command to "be alert." If anything, an intensification of consciousness is involved, with our minds fully open to the Spirit within and tuned in to the will of God.

I think we can say that the Spirit is able to help us communicate to God whenever we have *kawwanah*. Whenever we are as sincerely honest as we can be, the Spirit can work with our faltering words or even our best words, our poor expression or even our grandest, and translate it to the heart of God. His aid provides us the hope and the trust that God hears, that God can and will respond.

Keep Talking

A December 21, 1993, article in *USA Today* must have stunned the 20 percent of Americans who don't pray regularly. The article, titled "The Healing Power of Prayer," summarized the research reported in Larry Dossey's book *Healing Words: The Power of Prayer and the Practice of Medicine*. Dossey, who is not a member of any religious group, provides scientific evidence that prayer works. Formerly chief of staff at Medical City Dallas Hospital, Dossey documents that prayer for patients with high blood pressure, heart attacks, wounds, headaches and anxiety had observable benefits. The impact of prayer in his studies cannot be dismissed as simply the power of suggestion, either, because the patients were not made aware that prayers were being offered on their behalf!

You and I, of course, are not surprised. As we and our fellow believers have prayed, we have seen God do awesome things in the lives of all kinds of people in all kinds of situations and needs.

Mostly, though, we've seen the impact that talking to God has on our own lives. We know prayer energizes our spiritual growth. We know how it awakens us to God. We know it makes our life better, more meaningful, more purposeful.

So let's keep talking to God, but let's not be sloppy about it. Let's improve. Let's be mindful of the wondrous God we are talking to. Let's abandon inappropriate talk and develop prayer speech that is appropriate. Let's praise enthusiastically. Let's sing lustily. Let's confess openly. Let's request humbly. Let's speak honestly. Let's rely on the Spirit.

8

Needed Integration

Talk & Action

*A*s a child of the fifties who went to high school and college during the riot-torn sixties, I respond to the word *integration* with mental images of Rosa Parks, lunch-counter sit-ins, marches and Martin Luther King Jr.. I see U.S. marshals escorting a little black girl between jeering white faces into a formerly all-white elementary school in the South. I see black families risking their lives to end redlining and obtain homes in Cicero, near Chicago. I see a city water fountain marked "WHITE" on the wall above, with a long line of black men, women and children taking turns drinking heartily from it.

Eventually racial integration began to occur at all levels of American society. Integration quotas coupled with the determination of blacks brought significant breakthroughs in the numbers of black police officers, teachers, doctors, politicians and athletes. Integration continues today as African-Americans move through the ranks to become school board presidents, high-school principals, university professors, chief medical officers,

U.S. senators, NFL quarterbacks and baseball executives.

The painfully slow integration of African-Americans into the broader American society models profoundly the out-of-sync dynamics of our talk and our action. Ideally our talk and action should work in tandem, but as with integration, most often our actions lag considerably behind our talk.

Three separate constitutional amendments are dedicated to establishing the rights of African-Americans in the United States. Amendment Thirteen abolishes slavery, Amendment Fourteen proclaims the civil rights of all Americans, and Amendment Fifteen gives African-Americans the right to vote. In 1964 President Lyndon B. Johnson signed an equal rights bill barring discrimination in the workplace. Previous to that was the landmark Supreme Court decision in 1954 to overturn the "separate but equal" principle that had upheld segregation of schools in the South. These legal statements are our nation's talk. The long process of integrating African-Americans into all facets of American life is our action. We still have a long way to go.

The spiritual enterprise of talk ethics is not over when we have listened, controlled our talk and then spoken with grace and truth to both God and our fellow human beings. It all comes to nothing if our actions don't follow our good words. Reforming our talk into something that honors God requires one last step. We must act. We must do what we say. We must live as we say we believe. We must bring our deeds into line. With this, our spiritual strides in talk ethics come to full fruition.

Actions do speak louder than words. The use of federal marshals to ensure that Ruby Bridges could attend William Frantz Elementary School in New Orleans in the sixties blared all over the South, volumes louder than all the legislation that had said she could.

In Matthew 7:20 Jesus says, "By their fruit you will recognize them." This book has urged each of us to tend to the bushels of words that grow on our life's "tree." We must not ignore the cartloads of deeds our trees produce too. Spiritual growth involves making both our word-fruit and our deed-fruit the highest possible quality.

In this chapter, then, we will explore the variety of ways in which our actions relate to our talk and what we are to do about integrating them.

Doing the Words of Others

Integration of words does not actually begin with our own words. It begins with integrating the words of others into our life.

In its most basic form, integrating the words of others into our behavior is obedience. Our mother tells us to take out the trash. We do it—even if we are sixty and she's in a nursing home. Our boss tells to stay late to finish a project. We do it—even if we need to get home to fix supper. The police officer asks for our driver's license. We give it to him—even if we feel he has pulled us over for no good reason.

These aren't our words. However, as we submit to them, in effect they become our words. As our will conforms to the spoken will of others, we internalize the command and order ourselves to fulfill it. This is the nature of human beings. We are not computers like the laptop I am using right now. It has no will. It is software and hardware manipulating a binary command system at the touch of my fingers. It can't refuse to print the letters that make up this sentence. But if you were assisting me as a scribe, you could. You could say you don't agree with my words and put down your pencil. You could say you have the flu and need to go home now. Or you could tell yourself you will do your job and write. Then you would translate my words into your action.

Integrating the words of others into our actions does not actually require that a command be spoken. It can be unspoken. I can know that my mother wants me to take out the trash on Thursday evenings after supper because that is the family routine. It is a standing order whether voiced every week or not. Intuition can also tell me someone's command or desire for me. I may know my job and my boss so well that I can anticipate his command and volunteer to take on an extra job. If my staying late at his request pleases him, he will be bowled over by my knowing enough to volunteer.

Obedience engenders gratitude and goodwill. Whether the desires of others are voiced or unvoiced, when we integrate them into our own words and actions, we earn their respect even as we confirm our respect for them. The better we are able to honor the desires of others, the better we will get on in life.

However, we should consider the comment on obedience by William A.

Ward, a nineteenth-century theologian and leader of the Oxford Movement: "Every great person," he says, must learn not only "how to obey" but also "whom to obey, and when to obey."[1]

First Peter 2:13 tells Christians, "Submit yourselves for the Lord's sake to every authority instituted among men." Mostly the passage has in mind various governing authorities, because Peter believes that good citizens make good evangelists for the faith. Yet he also believes that Christians should recognize their social stations for the same purposes. Submissive Christian slaves imitate Christ and bring honor and respect to his name (2:18-25). So also Christian wives evangelize their pagan husbands through submission (4:1-6). For us as Christians, then, respectful obedience to governing and social authorities is paramount for the sake of the gospel. But Peter generalizes further. In 2:17 he tells us to "show proper respect to everyone" and lists fellow believers and God along with the king. Likewise, in Ephesians 5:21 Paul encourages us to "submit to one another out of reverence for Christ." In Ephesians 6:1 he specifies that children should obey their parents.

These key biblical passages make submission and obedience a full-time job for us. However, these commands cannot be universally applied, since the fact is that various authorities compete for our allegiance. Such conflicts make Christianity tough to live out. Does a young man sell drugs because his father tells him to? Does a believer in an anti-Christian country renounce God when the secret police torture her? Does an executive assistant illegally shred documents that would incriminate his employer?

We don't do these things, because the Bible makes it indisputably clear that our first loyalty is to God, even as we live out his will through the power of Christ in the kingdom of God that he established. All other biblical admonitions to submit are subordinate to this one. When any other authority tramples on the will of God, we must choose to do the will of God. This may mean taking a tough stand against a parent, a boss or even the government.

For centuries Christians have stood up and spoken out for God against opposition. Second-century martyrs like Ignatius and Polycarp can inspire us. Today high-school students "meet at the pole" for prayer, office workers take their coffee break to read their Bibles and pray, young people get involved in church and become Christians against their parents' wishes, and converts from Islam are excommunicated from their families and even jailed.

In the Old Testament, the Hebrew word *hear* when spoken by God, as in the often-used command "Hear, O Israel . . ." carries with it the idea of obedience. It is often teamed with the word *obey* to make this indisputable, as in Deuteronomy 6:3: "Hear, O Israel, and be careful to obey." We know that we cannot hear a command or request from God and remain passive. The only possibilities are active resistance and active response. Thus after Abraham has obeyed God's request to bring Isaac to the mountain of sacrifice, Genesis 22:18 says that Abraham "heard" (NIV "obeyed") God and prophesies that he and his descendants will be blessed. Abraham did not hear God's word until he obeyed it.

In the Gospels (Mt 22:15-22; Mk 12:13-17; Lk 20:20-26), Jesus examines a Roman denarius for the answer to an intriguing and potentially dangerous question: should Jews pay the Roman poll tax, an across-the-board tax on each person in Judea? Jesus' shrewd answer resounds with implications for us today: "Give to Caesar what is Caesar's and to God what is God's."

The fact that a likeness of Caesar was stamped on the coin suggests the unmitigated conclusion that Jews should pay the poll tax. The implication for us is that we should pay our taxes and support the government for the services it provides. Yet the second part of Jesus' answer recognizes the superior authority of God over us all. After all, whose image is stamped on us? Genesis 1:27 says it is God's. Jesus' point is that Caesar can have our money; God wants *us*. He wants our heart. He wants our soul. He wants and deserves our loyalty and obedience above everything and everyone else.

A wise rabbi, unnamed in *'Abot* 1:15, encapsulates the principle of obeying God as well as anything I have read. He says, "Do God's will as if it were your will." This is exactly right, isn't it? Because God created me with the capacity to refuse his will, doing his will requires incorporating what he wants into what I want and doing it.

Jesus portrays the stark reality of this in Matthew 7:21-23 by dramatizing the fate of many seemingly loyal disciples, people who drove out demons and did miracles in his name. He identifies their cries of "Lord, Lord" as empty because they have not been obedient to God. Only those who do "the will of my Father who is in heaven" will enter the kingdom of heaven, he decrees.

Without skipping a beat, in the very next paragraph (vv. 24-27) Jesus identifies his own words as the words of God that we should obey: "Therefore everyone who hears these words of mine and puts them into practice is like a wise man who built his house on the rock."

So God spoke his will profoundly in Jesus, and we need to pay special attention to incorporate his teaching into our lives. But God is able to speak his will to us in a variety of ways: through the Bible, a preacher, a friend, prayer, or even suffering and misfortune. As chapter five of this book emphasizes, we must listen carefully, but we must also *hear*. We must act out God's will.

Obedience is not the only way you and I integrate the words of others into our actions. Another way is best described as *influence*. We are influenced by others in many ways that don't involve obedience at all. We read books, newspapers and magazines. We view television and movies. We hear lectures and debates. We talk with Christian friends. These avenues of influence affect us more subtly than commands. Occasionally we can detect the direct impact of an influential source like this. Usually, however, they blend together into an indiscernible mass that grows into our will, our choices, our behavior.

As emphasized in chapter five, we need to allow the Holy Spirit to monitor these influences. If we do not listen to the discerning voice of the Holy Spirit, we can be influenced by ungodly sources and wind up doing things that are not only unbiblical but also immoral. Christians' murdering of abortion doctors and shooting up clinic reception areas in the name of God show just how contorted our wills can become by wrong and undiscerned influences. The Spirit can help us sort out these influences and keep us from going off the deep end.

As the words of others come to life in us, we must never lose sight of God and his will, his principles, his desires for our life. Obedience to others and influence from others should remain secondary to obedience to our Lord.

Doing Our Own Words

Consistency is the byword here. Our words and deeds should connect. We should not say one thing and do another. Rather, we keep our promises. We stand by our oaths. We are true to our word.

Chapter six emphasized how foundational truth is to talk ethics. Here we must recognize that the foundation of truth in speech extends to behavior and cannot be broken off or disconnected from it. The same goes for truth's twin in talk ethics, grace. Gracious speech, to be truly effective, must blossom into action.

Jimmy and Tammy Faye Bakker were smooth talkers. The right Christian words rolled off their lips like cream. In the name of Christ they were able to bilk millions from trusting believers. But their lives were a sham. Eventually the veneer was pulled back to reveal a ridiculously luxurious lifestyle, immoral relationships and scandalous business practices. These things were done not in the name of Christ but in the name of greed. A canyon existed between the Bakkers' talk and their action. Their hypocrisy became fodder for comedians and an embarrassment to all believers.

A more recent Christian scandal involved the revelation of a behind-the-scenes affair between singers Michael English and Marabeth Jordon, one of the beautiful voices in the group First Call. While singing lyrics about faithfulness to God, they were being patently unfaithful. When the news broke, Christian young people were devastated. How could they sing with such conviction while carrying on like that? I can tell you, youth sponsors at my church had their hands full counseling disillusioned kids that week.

Scandals of this sort abound today. And Jesus seemed to have plenty of examples in his own day from which to choose when he taught on this subject. He didn't name individuals, but he certainly put the finger on one particular religious group, the Pharisees.

Jesus castigates the Pharisees with one telling observation that he makes again and again in different forms. In Matthew 23:5 he says, "Everything they do is done for men to see." Even though they say they are serving God, the audience they are playing to is full of men and women. The Pharisees dress to impress: full, flowing robes (Mk 12:38), Big Gulp-size prayer boxes on their forearms and heads called phylacteries, extra-long bright blue cords on the four corners of their cloaks (Mt 23:5). God intended the phylacteries and cords to be personal and public reminders of a person's loyalty and reverence for him (Ex 13:9, 16; Num 15:37-39), but the Pharisees enlarge them and lengthen them for their own glory.

Jesus criticizes the Pharisees for their loud, lengthy prayers in the temple (Mk 12:40) and on the street corners (Mt 6:5). He ridicules them for sounding trumpets when they deliver their offerings (Mt 6:2) and counterpoints their habit of clanging their coins into the treasury box to a poor widow's quiet depositing of two small copper coins (Mk 12:42). Jesus is exasperated by the Pharisees' meticulous measurement of a tithe of spices, which were of enormous value, while they withheld from God justice, mercy and faithfulness (Mt 23:23). He says in Matthew 23:25 that they judiciously "clean the outside of the cup and dish, but inside . . . are full of greed and self-indulgence."

Probably what irks Jesus most about the Pharisees is how they claim to be champions of the law while their teaching regularly advocates skirting its weighty requirements. The Old Testament commands that all vows and oaths be kept and that they should be sworn in the name of God alone (Lev 19:12; Num 30:2; Deut 6:3; 23:21-23). The Pharisees advocate making oaths on the gold of the temple or even on the hairs of their head (Mt 5:36; 23:16-22) as an acceptable hedge should an oath be unfulfilled.

Instead of encouraging grown children to provide money to take care of their aging parents out of honor and respect, the Pharisees allow them to declare their money dedicated to God and keep it for themselves (Mk 7:9-13). They teach that a legal paper makes divorce acceptable to God, when the Old Testament says no such thing (Mt 5:31-32; 19:1-12; Deut 24:1).

The last straw is that they claim to know God yet pronounce that Jesus' comes from Beelzebub (Mt 12:24) and successfully plot his execution. In Matthew 23:33 Jesus identifies them as "a brood of vipers" and sarcastically ponders how they will escape hell.

Jesus cannot stomach the hypocrisy of the Pharisees, nor can he accept ours. Consistency is what he requires. He wants us to do our words. When you tell your boss you're coming in early to work on a report, be there!

When you tell your son you'll play catch with him after school, do it! If you say honesty is the best policy, live it out! That catchy Nike slogan applies to Christians: "Just do it!"

Consistency between our words and our actions is difficult. It is a constant struggle for all of us. It's so much easier to say the right things than to do them. In Romans 7 Paul captures brilliantly how you and I wrestle day by day to do what we believe and say we should do. Romans 7:19 reads, "For what I do is not the good I want to do; no, the evil I do not want to do—this I keep on doing."

Paul perceives that you and I cannot win this wrestling match for consistency without help. Fortunately, God has already sent us the help we need. "Thanks be to God," Paul says in verse 25, "through Jesus Christ our Lord!" In chapter 8 he goes on to explain how Jesus, because of conquering sin through his death and resurrection, deposits in us the "Spirit of God" (v. 9) to enable us to win this raging battle within.

Romans 7 helps us realize that the gap between our words and our actions is a reality for everyone. Even for Christians, with the power of the Spirit, shortening the distance is a slow process. It's because we all recognize our own failings at this that we so admire people of integrity, Christian or not. The police officer who won't take a bribe, the factory worker who produces quality workmanship despite lousy conditions and an uncaring head office, the doctor who chooses not to perform unnecessary surgery that would mean more money for her, the politician who doesn't take PAC money and who actually does what he says he will do in office: these are the people who stir our souls, giving us hope and confidence and inspiring us to live up to our own words.

A 1994 political cartoon proclaimed former president Jimmy Carter the best "appointee" in Bill Clinton's administration. Why is it that Carter is so often invited into sticky international crises to help negotiate peace—for example, in Haiti, North Korea, Serbia? It's not his political position. He holds no office. It's not his successful accomplishments as president. He was voted out of office after inflation hit 18 percent. Without doubt, it is his integrity. Disputing parties call for his help because he is a man of his word. They can trust him. He hears both sides. He offers solutions graciously. He tries to be fair. Not only that, he is one of the few politicians who not only say we must do something to help the poor but have actually done so (in his case through Habitat for Humanity).

Why is it that Billy Graham catapulted from a little-known revival speaker to the most respected religious figure in the United States? His books make the bestseller list; he provides spiritual counsel to president after president; he can speak to one billion people around the world in one broadcast, as he did on March 14, 1995.[2] Again, the answer is integrity. Graham embodies the common refrain "Practice what you preach." He has a huge organization that has always been run with integrity. He lives a life we all respect and admire.

These modern heroes of integrity should inspire each of us to *do* our words. Yet only One is eternally consistent in this way. The words of only One completely integrate with action. Only One can say, "My word is deed." God, whose words evoked creation, whose Word became flesh and dwelled among us, whose words never, ever fail—he is our ultimate model. Indeed, he is our source of power to seek consistency in our lives.

Our Words and Deeds Stand Together

The relationship between our words and our deeds in talk ethics, despite what has been said so far, should not be understood as a one-way street. Integrating our words into deeds is vital. However, words unconnected to deeds aren't always bad, nor are deeds unconnected to words. Sometimes they stand on their own. Like a red rose and a white carnation in a vase, they can stand separately and together at the same time. They don't have to be intertwined like vines or one submerged into the other like a bud and a flower.

A loving deed need not follow every time I tell my wife I love her. The pronouncement itself can stand on its own. Likewise, I can pick up my neighbors' papers when I notice they are on vacation even if I had not verbally offered to do so. The act can be independent of words.

James 2:12 tells us that both our words and our deeds should grow out of the same core Christian principle—loving our neighbor as ourselves: "Speak and act as those who are going to be judged by the law that gives freedom." In James the law of freedom (1:25) and the royal law (2:8) are the same thing, and James 2:8 states unequivocally that the royal law is "Love your neighbor as yourself." Furthermore, a key adverb in 2:12 (untranslated by the NIV) specifies that the manner in which we speak and act should follow the principle of neighbor love. Emphatically preceding both *speak* and *act* is a Greek word that is usually translated "thus" or "in such a way." James includes this word to reinforce the idea that the law of freedom he mentions as the yardstick of judgment is, in fact, the principle of neighbor love in verse 8.

So whether they are integrated or not, God assesses both our words and our deeds on how well they embody love for others. We are capable of showing love in both ways, but they aren't necessarily interchangeable. Sometimes true love involves determining whether a situation calls for us to do something or say something, or both, or neither.

Both our words and our deeds are fair game for God's judgment because both are outer extensions of our inner character. Both our words and our deeds result from decisions and choices we have made. Both are outward expressions of inward thoughts. Jesus articulates this point with six illustrations aimed at countering the superficial, overly literalistic interpretation of the law the Pharisees teach.

First, in Matthew 5:21-26 Jesus takes on the law against murder. The Pharisees teach that the sixth commandment is a statue that allows the civil court to prosecute one person for intentionally killing another human being. But Jesus says that from God's point of view murder can be *spoken* by disparagingly calling someone a fool, a geek or a moron. Further, the act of murder and the word of murder form a triad with the murderous thought that extends from anger.

At root, murder is a spiritual matter, not just a civil one. And so it is with adultery (5:27-30), divorce (5:31-32), breaking oaths (5:33-37), retaliating against insults (5:38-42) and treatment of enemies (5:43-47). We could name any word or deed and recognize an internal derivation. So our words and our deeds are reliable gauges of our character. God's judgment of us based on these two forms of expression is fair. Thus both require our attention, but doubly so our inner self, which triggers them both.

In the ideal world that Philo envisions, all three—thoughts, words and actions—should work together for good. He says, "For if our words correspond with our thoughts and intentions and our actions with our words and the three mutually follow one another, bound together with indissoluble bonds of harmony, happiness prevails, and happiness is wisdom pure of all falsehood."[3]

When everything is clicking spiritually, you and I can do this. Our absolutely right intentions can find expression in the right words and the right deeds. Since our spiritual guts are rotten with sin and evil, there's not much likelihood that we can do this very often, and certainly not without the help of the Spirit. Yet Philo's ideal corresponds to the spiritual goal for all of us who desire to be grow into the people we were created to be.

Philo recognizes also that this ideal correspondence of thought, word and deed is difficult to achieve in reality. In this light, he contemplates an intriguing question: how do our thoughts, words and deeds rank in terms of our capability to restrain them from sin?[4] Think about it yourself for a second. Let me help you by asking three further questions. How many murders have you committed? How many times have you slandered someone? How often have you become angry with others? The deeds are easily quantifiable, aren't they? The words might be quantifiable, if we stopped at the end of each day to total them. But the thoughts—aren't they beyond calculation?

By taking a personal inventory like this, we come to the same conclusion Philo did. He concludes that our deeds are the easiest to control and therefore ought be controlled flawlessly. We should also be able to control our words, he says, because they are all voluntary—even though we don't succeed at controlling them. Our thoughts, he believes, too often are able to circumvent our will because of outside influences.

Philo's last point seems questionable at first. But haven't you ever tried to will yourself to stop thinking about something? It doesn't work, does it? You have to distract yourself by counting sheep, watching television or doing something else. Simply willing not to think about something usually implants it in our mind even more. It can take root and grow even stronger.

Philo's observations help us to recognize how the battle to live according to the standard of love God unfolds and what are our best options for success.

Our first line of defense is to control our actions. As if guarding the wall of a fort, we should be able to limit our behavior pretty strictly from the onslaughts of sin. And it shouldn't be too difficult to identify the breaches in the wall and repair them by seeking forgiveness and renewed strength.

Words form the second line of defense, perhaps compared to the compound inside the fort. Sin can become a blur here and overrun us so quickly that we cannot easily identify what we are doing wrong. With ingenuity and determination, we can beat back the enemy, bandage our wounds and hold our own.

Our last line of defense, our thoughts, occupies the commander's headquarters. In here we are alone, fighting hand-to-hand against sin all day and all night. In the day we easily recognize sin and throw it out. But in the night—oh, in the night we cannot so easily discern sin's face from our own face in the mirror. Confusion and discouragement reign. Often we lose here because we forget that Christ is with us, *especially* here where we need so much more help. With his help we win. Too often, though, stalemate ties our hands.

As in the defense strategy for a fort, which deploys most of its forces to the wall and the fewest in the command post, with an intermediate number in the compound, our resistance to sin is strongest with our actions, next with our words and last in our thoughts.

God, I believe, has the right to expect our deeds to live up to his standard of love every day. He expects daily improvement in our words but recognizes how much more difficult this is than in our actions. He knows that in our thoughts we struggle every moment and that we will be overcome often—without his help, always.

Lest we marshal all our forces to the front—our deeds—and leave the command post empty, we should keep in mind the importance of success in our thoughts. Just as a commander is key for his troops' discipline and for the moral and ultimate victory, so every success against sin in our thoughts certainly multiplies into our words, and probably squares into our actions. Armies don't spend millions on officers' training for no reason. And so you and I must stand with Christ and fight for those thought victories, however small, as well as for the action victories and word victories.

So what do we do? We defend it all in the name of Christ, through the power of Christ, as best we can. Through his power we can overcome our worst thoughts. With his strength we can turn hurtful, evil words into gracious words of truth and encouragement. By his strength we can act with love toward those all around us.

Only Our Deeds Will Do

Words can do great things. They can bring a smile to one who is depressed. They can launch a career. They can reform a drug addict. But sometimes words, however gracious, however true, are not enough. They just don't cut it.

FTD florists have made millions with the slogan "Say it with flowers." Nike has done just as well with the slogan "Just do it." People know these slogans are true. Words alone simply ring hollow when action is called for.

James 2:14-17 pictures just this kind of situation. A person who is "without clothes and daily food" comes to our door. In the Jewish culture of James's time, most likely this means such a person would be wearing a ragged toga but lack the spare toga and coat (outer garment) that most people possessed. It would be like a street person wearing all that he owns, maybe a pair of worn-out jeans and a faded T-shirt.

This person is also malnourished, as many street people are. In those days people were paid at the end of each day for their labor. In fact, that's what a denarius was, a coin that functioned as minimum wage to compensate for one day's work. People used one day's earnings to purchase food for the next day. The person James describes is unable to do this. He or she has insufficient food from one day to the next.

When this poorly dressed, malnourished person comes to our door, James posits only two responses we could make: we can choose to comfort either with words or with food and clothing. One of these is patently unacceptable, while the other embodies the Christian principle of loving one's neighbor. James exposes the benevolent words "Go, I wish you well; keep warm and well fed" as detestable in this circumstance.

When we read these words, we may imagine that they are insincere sarcasm, accompanied by a snooty wave of the hand or muttered by an Ebenezer Scrooge. But actually James did not have in mind the insincere words of a scoundrel. The phrase "Go, I wish you well"—more literally, "Go in peace"—was a common Hebrew way of saying goodby (Judg 18:6; 1 Sam 20:42; 2 Sam 15:9). Jews today still say "Shalom" to convey this idea. It is unthinkable that James would picture a Jew saying this insincerely, since it assumes the concept that God will watch over the person to whom it is said, like saying "God bless."

Likewise, James assumes the encouragement "Keep warm and well fed" (2:16) to be well-intentioned. In fact, it is the utter sincerity of this verbal response that makes James's case. For no matter how well-meaning or sincere, mere words in this type of situation are useless. We may really believe that God does take care of the needy, and we could make a pretty good biblical case for it, but that doesn't help the person standing in front of us. "What good is it?" James asks.

Anything other than feeding and clothing the person is no good. Even the most gracious, sincere, encouraging words here are inappropriate and wrong. We must clothe and feed as God has given us the means to do. Nothing else expresses the graciousness and truth that spring from love.

First John 3:18 states in principle what James mostly illustrates. It says, "Dear children, let us not love with words or tongue but with actions and in truth." We know that this advice relates to what James is talking about because 1 John 3:17 visualizes a similar scenario: "If anyone has material possessions and sees his brother in need but has no pity on him, how can the love of God be in him?" John is not denying, any more than James, that love can and should be shown by words, but he is pointing out that words have limits. He underscores James's point that sometimes only deeds will do.

The word *pity* may make us think John is only encouraging us to have the right attitude of concern. He conceives of pity, however, as the motivator to concrete action. This is clear by what he says in verse 18.

John goes further in developing this principle than James. He views our loving actions as paramount because they grow out of the love of Christ, who historically and eternally acted on his love for humankind when he "laid down his life for us," as 1 John 3:16 says. Saying, thinking and feeling

Christ's love for humankind would not have accomplished what needed to be accomplished. Jesus' self-sacrificing love publicly displayed on the cross is what we need to deal with our otherwise irresolvable predicament of sin.

The supreme act of love is to sacrifice our life for the life of another. Most of us can say we would do this for our children or our spouse. But would we give our life for someone we don't know or even dislike? People do that too, rushing into burning buildings or diving into rivers. John, however, is not necessarily talking about heroic acts. He's saying that every day our lives teem with opportunities to imitate Christ's sacrificial love and that taking action in these opportunities establishes our claim to be Christian.

Maybe it means something as simple as handing over our change or our lunch to a street person, stopping to help a stranded motorist or giving time to help a neighbor paint her house. Maybe something more serious is involved, like donating a kidney to a brother or sister or putting our life at risk to bring the gospel to Zaire.

Talk, however gracious and true it might be, can never be equated with self-sacrifice. Little wonder, then, that Christ spoke so little at his trial and crucifixion. Similarly, Jesus' statement in Matthew 7:21 is not surprising: "Not everyone who says to me, 'Lord, Lord,' will enter the kingdom of heaven, but only he who does the will of my Father who is in heaven." And we can now appreciate the parable of the sheep and the goats (Mt 25:31-46), in which those who did not feed the hungry or clothe the needy are condemned when the King says, "Whatever you did not do for one of the least of these, you did not do for me."

So when the situation calls for self-sacrifice, we must discard words in favor of appropriate loving action. Nothing else will do.

The Perfect Integration

Balancing words and deeds is no simple task. The quest for integration, obedience, integrity, consistency, independence puts us behind the eight ball daily. How do we know what to do when? Feelings of defeat and inadequacy may overwhelm us. Maybe abject honesty with our sinfulness in this area of integrating words and deeds is good for us. But encouragement and motivation to succeed just a little more each day with our words and deeds are readily available in the person of Jesus Christ.

Jesus faced temptation in all areas as we do, including the struggle to blend words and deeds, and succeeded (Heb 4:15). No gap existed between his words and deeds. They were perfectly integrated. No rebellion occurred in him. He obeyed the will of the Father. His words and deeds were perfectly consistent. His words and deeds stand up to scrutiny, together or separate. He also knew when to shut up and act.

Not just Christians recognize this about Jesus. He receives worldwide respect outside of Christendom for his unparalleled integration of words and actions. While watching a 1994 Christmas special, the thirteenth annual NBC *Christmas in Washington,* I was stunned by what I heard. In a country that bans Nativity scenes from courthouse squares, and with President Clinton, Hillary Rodham Clinton and many members of the Washington, D.C., establishment in attendance, the host of this hour of Christmas celebration introduced the evening with these words:

> We celebrate a season which in name is Christian but is embraced by hundreds and millions of people of other religions or actively of no religion at all, because the spirit of unselfish service personified by the life and teaching of Jesus Christ touches the inner consciousness and hope of every man and every woman in every part of the earth.

She's right. An advertising slogan may say, "I wanna be like Mike [Michael Jordan]." But down deep, people really want to be like Jesus Christ, whether they know it or not. For people who have never heard of Christ at all, you and I can bring him to life in our own lives in a way that will stir their latent desire to be know him and be like him too. Because of Christ's power in us, we too can make our lives such a powerfully balanced integration of loving words and deeds that people will be drawn to us. They will see Christ in us and want him too.

Integrating our words and actions, then, goes far beyond ethics or morality. It has to do with our witness to the reality of Jesus Christ. If he is real, then in a world like ours, our well-balanced words and deeds should stand out above the crowd. This is a kind of witness to the power of Christ that brooks no argument. Christ makes us better people, in word and in deed.

Epilogue

Not long ago I learned a new lesson in speech ethics. It involved something I said to my son Gavin. He was getting his gear together for his team's Little League game one evening. Because I couldn't attend the game, I wanted to send him off with words of encouragement. Jokingly, I said, "Don't hit any home runs tonight, OK?" Little did I know the positive and negative effect of these words from Dad on a ten-year-old.

To my chagrin, upon returning home that evening, I was told that Gavin had hit a ball so far that he could have walked to the plate from third. But what did he do? He stopped at third and would not budge despite the urgings of the third-base coach. Later the coach told me Gavin was adamant that he would not break his promise not to hit a home run that night.

The power of words goes far beyond our imaginings. We need to be so careful and prudent with them. My words provided Gavin confidence, but at the same time they held him back from a personal achievement he could have treasured. That was the last thing I really wanted.

Was this devastating to Gavin? Actually it didn't bother him a bit. He was completely matter-of-fact about it. He knew he would hit other home runs, even though he didn't that year. But it bothers me, because my words were too flippant. It makes me want to do better next time.

I guess that's the bottom line for all of us. We can do better. We can make our words instruments of peace and fulfillment, of honesty and tact. We can learn from our mistakes to be more controlled, more discerning, more loving. We can edge daily toward spiritual maturity as we study God's Word and allow the Spirit of Christ within to teach us and lead us in this crucial area of speech ethics.

I recall a recent time when I did better with our other son. Kyle was pondering what he should do for his fifth-grade science project. Would he do an experiment like last year's, or something quite different? He was settling on some investigation involving electronics. He is an ambitious young man, so I was shocked when he told me he thought he would like to make a flashlight. When I questioned him, he said what he really wanted to make was a robot, but he was afraid he couldn't do it. He had talked to some of his classmates about building a robot from a design in a book he had seen, but they thought he was nuts. I asked him if he wanted just to do a project and get it over with, or if he wanted to learn something from an achievement he could be proud of. He chose the latter, and RB-3 was born in our basement two months later.

Our words can do incredible things when we get them right. Through God's power they can reach to the depths of others and draw out the best in them. Our words play a vital role in God's work of building people into all they can be. It's mind-boggling to think that we participate in God's providential care of people in this way, but we do. We really do. It should make us fall to our knees daily and plead with God to keep us alert to people's needs and hurts, conscious of their potential and spiritually selective of our words and actions toward them. May he bless our conversations daily!

As Christians we are committed to being like Jesus, and no one offers a better example of talk ethics than he does. He could prick the heart of a callused Samaritan woman. He could chastise a rabbi like Nicodemus. He could heal the only son of a destitute widow without being asked. He could treat blind men, lepers and Gentiles with dignity. He could play with children and censure pompous religious leaders. He could challenge off-base teaching and egotistical leadership with provocative words of judgment. His words could stop Peter from violence, yet bring violence down upon himself to accomplish God's loving purposes for sinful humankind. He prayed to God for counsel and acted on it. All his conversations were God-controlled, God-centered.

This is our goal in talk ethics: to be like him. He shows us that our speech can be used effectively in God's will. He shows us how it is done. He supplies us the resurrection power of the Spirit to do it.

Can we do better in our speech tomorrow than we did today? Indeed we can. This book invites you to be open to dramatic changes in your life. Maybe it will affect how you relate to one person, or, step by step, how you relate to everyone. At the very least, I trust this book has helped you become aware of just how critical your talk is in your walk with God each day.

May God bless your every word, even as I trust he will bless the words in this book written for his glory and the glory of his kingdom.

Notes

Introduction

[1]Sissela Bok, *Lying* (New York: Quartet Books, 1978), pp. xix, 289. *Encyclopedia of Philosophy* is edited by Paul Edwards and published by Macmillan (1967).

[2]J. B. Pritchard, ed., *Ancient Near Eastern Texts* (Princeton, N.J.: Princeton University, 1969), p. 412.

[3]William Kelly Simpson, ed., *The Literature of Ancient Egypt* (London: Yale University Press, 1973), p. 412.

Chapter 1: Speech Is Powerful

[1]*Leviticus Rabbah* 33:1.

[2]Plutarch, a first-century A.D. moral philosopher, includes four different versions of the rabbinic tongue story in his writings (*Moralia* 1.38b; 2.146f; 6.506c; 15.89). Diogenes Laertius (1.105), a third-century A.D. Greek writer, attributes a similar tongue story to Anarchis, a sixth-century B.C. Scythian prince.

[3]Menander 560k (Loeb Classical Library).

[4]*Enconium on Helen* 14.

[5]*Šabbat* 88b; *Yoma* 72b.

[6]In his important two-volume work *The Theology of the Old Testament,* trans. J. A. Baker (London: SCM Press, 1967), 1:69-70, Walther Eichrodt states that words "virtually have a life of their own; they are like independent beings waiting their opportunity to invade reality. And even when this is denied them they remain

dangerous for a long time, like a long-forgotten mine in the sea, or a grenade in a ploughed field." Gerhard von Rad (*Old Testament Theology*, trans. D. M. G. Stalker, 2 vols. [Edinburgh: Oliver & Boyd, 1965], 2:80-85) and E. Jacob (*Theology of the Old Testament* [London: Hodder & Stoughton, 1958], p. 127) make similar statements. Anthony Thiselton ("The Supposed Power of Words in Biblical Writings," *Journal of New Testament Studies* 25 [1974]: 283-99) exposes the extent to which this view pervades Old Testament theology and calls it into question.

[7]In James Barr's influential book *The Semantics of Biblical Language* (Oxford: Oxford University Press, 1961), pp. 129-40, he chooses the very word *dābār*, ("word") to discredit the practice of combining alternate meanings of words, like "word" and "thing" for *dābār*, into one composite meaning, as von Rad in fact does in one of his arguments for the independent power of words (*Old Testament Theology*, 2:81). In "The Symbolism of Names in the Old Testament," *Bulletin of the John Rylands Library* 52 (1969-1970): 11-30, Barr dismantles the common assumption that people's names in the Old Testament had inherent power—another idea expressed by von Rad (*Old Testament Theology*, 2:83). Among Barr's points are that the only names with power are associated with powerful people or gods, which indicates a connection between the person and the influence of the name, and most names that can be translated into meaningful phrases say something about God rather than about the person himself, which indicates a theological or providential connection to the influence of the name.

[8]Eichrodt, *Theology of the Old Testament*, 2:70. See also John Gray, *I and II Kings*, Old Testament Library (London: SCM Press, 1970), 263; Sheldon H. Blank, "The Curse, Blasphemy, the Spell and the Oath," *Hebrew Union Theological Annual* 23 (1950-1951): 94; Arthur Cundall, *Judges*, Tyndale Old Testament Commentary (London: Tyndale, 1968), p. 183; George Foot Moore, *Judges*, International Critical Commentary (Edinburgh: T & T Clark, 1895), p. 373.

[9]Blank, "Curse, Blasphemy," p. 94; J. R. Porter, *Leviticus* (London: Cambridge University Press, 1976), p. 154; Martin Noth, *Leviticus*, Old Testament Library (London: SCM Press, 1965), p. 141; N. H. Snaith, *Leviticus and Numbers*, New Century Bible Commentary (London: Nelson, 1967), p. 130; and J. A. Motyer, "Curse," in *The Illustrated Bible Dictionary*, ed. J. D. Douglas et al., 3 vols. (Leicester, England: Inter-Varsity Press; Wheaton, Ill.: Tyndale House, 1980), 1:319.

[10]H. C. Brichto, *The Problem of the Curse in the Hebrew Bible*, Society of Biblical Literature Monograph 13 (Philadelphia: Society of Biblical Literature, 1963), p. 121.

Chapter 2: Daily Speech Sins: Careless Hurt

[1]In the Apocrypha, Sirach 22:6 says, "Like music in a time of mourning is inopportune narration." Theognis, a fifth-century B.C. Greek poet, says, "Never let

us laugh in the joy of our good fortune, Cyrnus, when we sit beside a mourner" (lines 1217-18 [Loeb Classical Library]).

[2]*Moralia* 8.632d, 631c.

[3]*Discourses* 4.12.17.

[4]*Nicomachean Ethics* 2.6.1-20, 7.1-9.9.

[5]Rabbi Hana ben Raba in *Šabbat* 33a.

[6]*Megilla* 25b.

[7]*Pesiqta* 3a.

[8]*Moralia* 6.506f-507b.

[9]In 1953 Julius Rosenberg and his wife Ethel were executed as spies for supplying the Soviet Union with secrets for constructing the atomic bomb.

[10]*Moralia* 6.503d.

[11]*Exodus Rabbah* 31:9.

[12]Sirach 27:17; 19:5; 19:12-16.

[13]*Moralia* 6.507c-f.

[14]*Moralia* 6.509a.

[15]*Enchiridion* 33.2.

[16]Amen-em-Opet in *The Literature of Ancient Egypt,* ed. William Kelly Simpson (London: Yale University Press, 1973), pp. 262-63. This was written between 1300 and 1000 B.C.

[17]*Works* 330-334. Hesiod dates in the sixth century B.C. with Homer. Other Greek writers who mention orphans include Demosthenes (*Orations* 18.192), Euripides (fr. 130), Epictetus (*Discourses* 1.26.13-15) and Plutarch (*Moralia* 1.35c-d).

[18]*Peace* 743-47.

[19]*To Democles* 29.

[20]The rabbis comment in *Genesis Rabbah* 24:7 that to insult a fellow human being is to insult God, in whose image all are made.

[21]*De Decalogo* 1-3.

[22]Similar teaching on how to handle being mocked appears in Greek and Roman literature. Different pieces of advice from Seneca (*De constantia sapientis [ME]* 2.1-3; 3.2; 12.3; 13.5; *De ira [ME]* 3.43.1-5), Epictetus (*Enchiridion* 42) and Plutarch (*Moralia* 1.35d) can be condensed into "Bear it with gentleness, be secure in yourself, and in effect receive no insult at all."

[23]*'Abot* 4:3; 1:6.

[24]Sirach 29:19-21.

[25]*Aboth de Rabbi Nathan,* trans. Judah Goldin, Yale Judaica Series (New Haven, Conn.: Yale University Press, 1955), 7, p. 4; 1, p. 7.

[26]*Pesaḥim* 113b.

[27]*De Agricultura* 17; *De Migratione Abrahami* 210; *Legum Allegoriae* 3.124.

[28]*Nicomachean Ethics* 2.7.11-13.

[29]*De ira* 2.34.5.

Chapter 3: Daily Speech Sins: Shades of Falsehood

[1]*Šabbat* 104a.

[2]The story is reported by Maureen Riegert, "The Cost of Integrity" *APU Life* (Azusa Pacific University), Spring 1992, p. 14.

[3]Charles Colson, "Ethics: The Inward Quest," *APU Life*, Spring 1992, p. 4.

[4]"Surprising Truths About Why People Lie," *USA Today*, January 9, 1992.

[5]*De Ebrietate* 70-71; *De Posteritate Caini* 101.

[6]Francis Schaeffer, *True Spirituality* (Wheaton, Ill.: Tyndale House, 1971), pp. 100-101.

[7]*Pesiqta* 118a.

[8]*Midraš Psalms* 12:2.

[9]*Deuteronomy Rabbah* 5:10; *Leviticus Rabbah* 26:2; *Numbers Rabbah* 19:2.

[10]*Antidosis* 18-19.

[11]*Šabbat* 33a (croup); *'Arakin* 16a; *Numbers Rabbah* 16:6 (leprosy); *Deuteronomy Rabbah* 6:8-10; *Leviticus Rabbah* 17:3 (plagues), *Deuteronomy Rabbah* 5:10 (drought, Shechinah).

[12]*Genesis Rabbah* 20:1.

[13]*Deuteronomy Rabbah* 5:10; 6:14; *Leviticus Rabbah* 26:2; *Numbers Rabbah* 19:22.

[14]The Greek words discussed here are *katalalos, blasphmia, loidoros, diabolos.*

[15]Matthew 7:1-5; Luke 6:37-42; John 7:24; 8:15-16; Romans 2:1; 14:4; 1 Corinthians 4:5; 5:12. James, in fact, appeals to it in at least two other contexts, in James 2:8 and 1:25, referred to respectively as the "royal" law and the law of "freedom."

[16]Diogenes Laertius *Lives* 1.104 tells this of Anacharsis, a Scythian prince.

[17]Dennis Kelly, "Cheating Is a Basic College Course," *USA Today*, May 6, 1991.

[18]*Tosepta, b. Kamma* 7:8.

[19]Matthew 24:4-24 (Mk 13:5-6; Lk 21:8); 1 Corinthians 3:18; 6:9; 15:13; 2 Corinthians 11:3; Galatians 6:7; Ephesians 4:14; Colossians 2:4-8; 2 Thessalonians 2:3; 1 Timothy 1:4; 2:14; 6:4; 2 Timothy 2:23; 3:13; Titus 3:9; 1 Peter 3:10; 2 Peter 2:13; 1 John 2:26; 3:7; 2 John 7; Jude 16. Paul does all he can to dissociate himself and the gospel from this kind of flattery and deceptive speaking (1 Cor 1:18—2:16; 2 Cor 2:17; 4:2; Gal 1:10; 1 Thess 2:3, 5-6).

[20]*Soṭa* 41b.

[21]*Tosepta, Soṭa* 7:16.

[22]*Moralia* 1.5b, 13b.

[23]*Quomodo adulescens poetas audire debeat, Moralia* 1.48e-74e.

[24]*Moralia* 1.49a-b.

[25]Ibid. 1.5b, 13b.

[26]*Legum Allegoriae* 3.182.

[27]Colson, "Ethics," p. 5.

[28]*ʿArakin* 16a; *Ketubot* 17a.

[29]*Republic* 389b; 382d.

[30]Sennacherib's boasting comes up in 2 Kings 18—19, 2 Chronicles 32 and Isaiah 10 and 15. It is also mentioned in Tobit 1:18 and Sirach 48:18 in the Apocrypha.

[31]*Soṭa* 47b. See also *Lamentations Rabbah* 23; *Ecclesiastes Rabbah* 10:1; *Leviticus Rabbah* 20:2, 10.

[32]*Sanhedrin* 93b.

[33]The saying is identical in Luke 14:11 and 18:4, and nearly so in Matthew 23:12. One can see the notion rephrased in Matthew 11:23 (Mk 10:15; Lk 18:17), Luke 16:15, Romans 12:16, 2 Corinthians 11:7, 1 Timothy 6:17, James 4:10 and 1 Peter 5:6.

[34]Luke 6:24-26; 12:21; 16:5-19; Matthew 23:1-36 (Mk 12:37-40; Lk 20:45-47); 1 Timothy 6:17-19; 2 Peter 2:10, 17.

[35]Romans 1:30 (2 Tim 3:2); 3:27; 12:3, 16; 1 Corinthians 1:26-29; 3:21-23; 4:7; 5:6; 15:10; 2 Corinthians 11:16-17; 12:4; Galatians 6:3; Ephesians 2:8-9; Philippians 2:3; 3:9-10; Colossians 2:18; 2 Timothy 3:1-4.

[36]*De Specialibus Legibus* 1.10.

[37]*Nicomachean Ethics* 4.7.10-13.

Chapter 4: The Key to the Ethics of Talk: Control

[1]Joshua ben Levi, *Leviticus Rabbah* 16:5.

[2]*De Confusione Linguarum* 37.

[3]*Berakot* 24b; *Megilla* 18a; *Midraš Psalms* 19:1.

[4]*Moralia* 3.239d.

[5]*Moralia* 3.208c.

[6]*Moralia* 6.515a.

[7]*Frogs* 2.373.

[8]*Moralia* 1.41d.

[9]Translations are divided about whether the phrase "world of evil" should be take as the subject of "is appointed," as I have, or as an apposition to "the tongue is a fire." It depends on where one places a comma, and punctuation is not included in ancient New Testament manuscripts. Most scholars agree that "world of evil" should go with "is appointed," as I have assumed. However, not many modern translations have incorporated this scholarly consensus. The problem here has been noted as one of the most vexing in all the New Testament by Martin Dibelius, *James* (Philadelphia: Fortress, 1976), p. 193.

Chapter 5: A Vital Bridge: Listening

[1]Ptah-Hotep, in *Ancient Near Eastern Texts*, p. 414.

[2]Walter Wangerin, *Ragman and Other Cries of Faith* (San Francisco: Harper & Row, 1984), pp. 126-27.

[3]*Moralia* 1.39b.

[4]*Moralia* 6.502d.

[5]*Moralia* 6.502c.

[6]*Moralia* 1.48d.

[7]Deuteronomy 5:1; 6:3-4; 9:1; 20:3; 1 Samuel 12:14-15; Amos 3:1; 4:1; 5:1; Micah 1:2; 3:1,7; Malachi 2:2.

[8]'*Abot* 6:9.

[9]'*Abot* 3:9, 14.

[10]*Epistulae Morales* 27:7-8.

[11]*De Somnis* 2.264; *De Congressu Eruditionis Gratia* 53; *De Vita Contemplativa* 31.75-82.

[12]Revelation and the Gospels give us so many records of Jesus' saying this that we can assume he said it often. See Matthew 11:15; 13:43; 25:29; Mark 4:23; 7:16; Luke 8:8; 14:35; Revelation 2:7, 11, 17, 28; 3:6, 13, 22; 12:9.

[13]See also John 7:16-18; 8:26, 51-52; 10:27-28; 12:49; 14:10, 31; 17:6-8.

Chapter 6: Twin Goals: Truth & Grace

[1]*Quod Deterius Potiori Insidiari Soleat* 40; *De Migratione Abrahami* 79-81; *De Vita Mosis* 2:127-29; *De Somnis* 2:269; *Quod Deterius Potiori Insidiari Soleat* 126-29.

[2]*De Migratione Abrahami* 80-81.

[3]*Quis Rerum Divinarum Heres sit* 14.

[4]*Legatio ad Gajum* 245.

[5]'*Abot* 2:13. See also '*Abot* 3:10; 6:6; *Genesis Rabbah* 73:12; *Ecclesiastes Rabbah* 1:16.

[6]*Genesis Rabbah* 67:3. This is a fascinating passage about how the mouth is one of the three organs, along with the hand and the foot, that a person normally controls and for which he is normally responsible.

[7]I expand here on three reasons for lying cited in "Lies, Lies, Lies," *Time,* October 5, 1992.

[8]*Republic* 382d, 389b.

[9]See Sissela Bok, *Lying* (New York: Quartet, 1978).

[10]In addition to the New Testament passages cited, see Romans 15:14; Ephesians 5:11; 1 Thessalonians 5:14; 2 Thessalonians 3:14-15; Titus 1:9, 13; 2:15.

[11]'*Abot* 1:18.

[12]*Laws* 730c.

[13]*Moralia* 1:49a.

[14]*Tosepta, Šebi'it* 3:6.

[15]*Sanhedrin* 92a.

[16]The word *tested* in Psalm 119:140 usually has a technical usage for refining gold or silver. See also Psalm 12:6; 18:30; Proverbs 30:5.

[17]2 Corinthians 6:7; Galatians 2:5; Ephesians 1:13; Colossians 1:5; 1 Timothy 2:7.

[18]Romans 10:16; Galatians 5:7; 1 Peter 1:22; 2 Peter 1:12; 1 John 3:19; 2 John 1, 4; 3 John 4.

[19]*To Nicanor* 22.

[20]*Enchiridion* 33.6.

[21]*Pro Balbo* 5:12.

[22]*Nicomachean Ethics* 14.7.6-8 (1126b30-1127a8).

[23]Although not attributed to Jesus, James 5:12 is widely acknowledged by scholars to reflect Jesus' teaching. Upon close examination, it also affirms direct honesty more clearly than Matthew 5:12, which, strictly translated, allows a doubled *yes* or *no* answer rather than swearing.

Chapter 7: Spiritual Communication: Talking to God

[1]In Tony Castle, *The Hodder Book of Christian Quotations* (London: Hodder & Stoughton, 1982), p. 190.

[2]The casuistic practices of swearing on anything but God's name is reflected in Jesus' recommendation not to swear at all. See Mathew 5:33-37; 23:16-22; James 5:12.

[3]The concept of blasphemy in the Old Testament encompasses a cluster of words including *revile, scorn, taunt, despise* and *curse.*

[4]The Bible's heavy coverage of this situation highlights its significance. See 2 Kings 18:17—19:37; 2 Chroncles 32:1-22; 36:18-22; 37:10-29.

[5]Acts 13:45; 18:6; 26:11; 1 Timothy 1:19-20; 6:1; Titus 2:5; 2 Peter 2:2.

[6]In Castle, *Hodder Book of Christian Quotations,* p. 191.

[7]1QH 1:28-31.

[8]1QS 11:9-10.

[9]*Genesis Rabbah* 13:15.

[10]*Midraš Psalms* 88:1.

[11]Check these out: Psalm 5:11; 9:1-2, 11; 13:16; 18:49; 27:6; 28:7; 30:4, 10-12; 32:11; 33:1-3; 35:28; 42:11; 43:4-5; 45:16-17; 47:1, 7; 48:1, 10; 51:15; 52:9; 56:4; 57:7-9; 59:6; 61:8; 63:3-5; 66:8; 67:1-7; 68:5; 69:30-36; 71:22-24; 75:1, 9; 79:3; 81:1-5; 89:1; 92:1-4; 95—100; 101:1; 105:1-3; 106:1-3, 47; 107:1-2; 108:1-6; 111—113; 117; 118:1-4; 135:1-4; 136; 138; 145:21; 146—150.

[12]Exodus 15:1-17; 1 Kings 4:32; Luke 1:46-56, 67-79. David was the writer of many of the Psalms.

[13]Romans 1:8-9; 1 Corinthians 1:4; 2 Corinthians 13:7-9; Ephesians 1:15-19; Philippians 1:3-10; Colossians 1:3-5; 1 Thesssalonians 1:2; 3:9-10; 2 Thessalonians 1:3,11; 2:13.

[14]In Castle, *Hodder Book of Christian Quotations,* p. 191.

Chapter 8: Needed Integration: Talk & Action
[1]In Castle, *Hodder Book of Christian Quotations,* p. 172.
[2]*Christianity Today,* April 24, 1995, pp. 36-37.
[3]*De Praemiis et Poenis* 81. See also *De Vita Mosis* 2:138-41.
[4]*De Mutatione Nominum* 240-44.